KV-513-450

Contents

CONTENTS

Illustrations

Our grateful thanks to Timothy Goodwin who did
the general historical research from prehistoric
to medieval times. We owe him much for his flair
and knowledge, and enjoyed working with him.

Suzanne Ebel and Doreen Impey.

Introduction

The cycling trips in this book are based on thirteen different centres in the Cotswolds, all places of reasonable size. We have put the centres for ease of reference in alphabetical order. And at the end of these trips are five week-end trips, longer in mileage and with more things to see, which are also listed alphabetically.

Some of the journeys we have written about will take you beyond the actual area of the Cotswolds – to Stratford-upon-Avon, for instance, or to Evesham – although they begin in Cotswold country. This is because there are interesting and beautiful things to see just beyond the Cotswolds, and while you are in the district it's pleasant to see all you can.

Neither of us knew the Cotswolds when we started to write this book. We'd visited one or two of its most famous towns, but the Cotswold country itself was an unexplored one for us both.

Since then we've visited over two hundred little villages and small towns. We've walked through the high grass of churchyards in the rain, peered through brambles to see the ruined doorway of what was once a manor of the nobility. We've talked to farmers and curators, looked at exquisite gardens, picknicked by rivers whose names seem to belong in Tolkein – the Windrush, the Evenlode. Almost all our travels have been at the top of the tourist season. Yet, the moment we left the main roads we went for miles without meeting a soul. Once or twice we met a hare!

The wonderful thing about the Cotswolds even now in the 1970s is that they stay so beautiful, and that English history can be found so easily. Often you will have to cycle to the little church, because it is *there* that the real past has been preserved. The portraits in stone or brass. The faint, menacing doom paintings. The alabasters. And the sculpted faces who look at you, often ironically, from the walls or who kneel piously beside their overdressed wives, seem curiously modern with their long hair and beards.

A bicycle is the perfect way to tour the Cotswolds. Yes, you'll sometimes have to push your bicycle up a hill, but you'll spin down the other side. And the view at the top, or the treasures you'll find there, will always be worth the effort.

We used Ordnance Survey maps on every journey, and have given the numbers of the maps you'll need. They're so exact that it is simple to follow them.

All the time we travelled we never found an unclassified road which was busy. In fact we went for hours without seeing a car at all. What we did see were birds and rabbits, wild flowers and magnificent trees, swift rivers, honey-coloured villages, and views that were touching in their beauty and peacefulness. And we found the Cotswolds. Which was what we were looking for.

Suzanne Ebel and Doreen Impey.

Choosing your bicycle

Whether you are an experienced cyclist who wishes to buy a new cycle, a former cyclist who wants to recapture the joys of cycling, or someone who has never owned a cycle before, it is helpful to go to a shop displaying the N.A.C. and M.C.T. sign. This means that the dealer is a member of the National Association of Cycle and Motor Cycle Traders, and you can be sure that he will give you helpful advice and good after-sales service. He will help you choose the bicycle best suited to you, especially regarding the following important points.

The Frame
The frame must be the right size for you, since it is the frame size, not the size of the wheels, which ensures comfort, safety and efficiency of the machine. There are many different frame shapes, from the conventional frame with large wheels (26 in.) and gears ranging from 5 to 10 speeds which are ideal for touring to the small wheel cycles more suitable for commuting in-town and for shorter distances. A small person needs a bicycle with an 18 in. frame or less, a big person one of up to 24 in. The correct test of the size of the frame is that when seated on the cycle, with your hands resting on the handlebar grips you should be able to touch the ground with the balls of your feet. Small-wheeled cycles offer more adjustment of the handlebar and saddle so that the frame size is not quite so critical as it is on conventional designs.

8

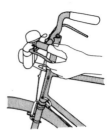
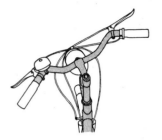

Stirrup Brakes   **Flat Handlebar**

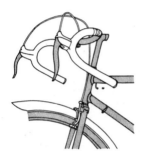

Dropped Handlebar

Saddle types

CHOOSING YOUR BICYCLE

The Handlebar
A comfortable riding position can be obtained with a flat, wide handlebar while for touring purposes the well-known dropped handlebar is good in hilly country. This should not be adjusted so as to force the rider into a head-down position; more cycling skill is needed with this type of handlebar, and care should be taken to see that the brakes are adjusted to be easily accessible.

The Saddle
The use to which you are mainly going to put your machine should determine your choice of saddle, of which there is a wide range of types. Here again, your N.A.C. and M.C.T. dealer will give you the best possible advice.

The Brakes
There are four kinds of braking system; the calliper or scissor system, and the pull-up or stirrup-system; these operate on the side rims and wheel rims respectively. Then there are the internal expanding type which operates on the hub, and the coaster hub or back-pedalling type. The choice of braking system is governed by the kind of wheel fitted to the machine. It is vital that, if you carry out any adjustments to your bicycle, you make sure that braking efficiency has not been adversely affected.

The Gears
There are two types of gear system; the hub gear is totally enclosed, and operates inside the hub, while the derailleur is an external system giving a wider choice of gear ratios. You should consider your choice of gear system at the time you buy your machine, as it is difficult and costly to change afterwards.

Ready for the Road
Every machine allows for certain adjustments to the handlebar and the saddle – be sure that yours is adjusted for maximum comfort and efficiency. Check that your lighting system is working properly, and carry a small tool kit and tyre repair outfit for roadside maintenance. The driving chain should be properly adjusted and brakes in perfect working order. And don't forget your pump!

Running Cost and Maintenance
The cost of running a bicycle is remarkably low, and is one of the bicycle's great advantages. The cost averages less than £1·25 for 3,000 miles of cycling.

The cycle only needs basic maintenance to keep it in good condition:

Lubrication. This is always needed where metal moves against metal – e.g. on all hinged joints on brake levers and rods, head races, wheel hub, bottom bracket, and pedal bearings, chain, free wheel and variable speed hub. Never put lubricants on wheel rims or brake rubbers. If you do, your brakes won't work at all.

Lighting. If you have battery lighting make sure that you never go out with weak batteries. If you have dynamo lighting make sure that your dynamo is properly adjusted. Both front and rear lamps must be cleaned regularly, and a good cyclist will carry spare bulbs. The reflector should be clean and pointing squarely to the rear.

Brakes. Check your brake blocks and replace them before they become badly worn. Adjust your brakes so that the blocks are close to the rim but clear of it when the brakes are off. Make sure that the closed end of the brake shoes is always facing in the direction of travel.

Front and Rear Hubs. Adjust cones to avoid 'shake' and keep wheel nuts tight.

Chain. Adjust so that 'up-and-down' play midway does not exceed $\frac{3}{4}$ in.

Pedals. They should rotate freely and without 'shake'.

Spokes. Any broken, slack, or bent spokes should be attended to by your service dealer.

Steering Head. Check for 'shake' and adjust if necessary.

Tyres. Keep them pumped up hard. Check regularly for tread wear and cuts in side walls.

Bottom Bracket. Keep adjusted so as to avoid 'shake'.

The Highway Code

Bicycles are 'vehicles' and subject to the law. Cyclists should study the Highway Code, which briefly sets out what every cyclist should know.

Important Points Include:
(1) That a cycle should have two effective braking systems, one on each wheel.

(2) That the rider must be able to give 'audible' warning of approach, and that a bell is a recognised warning sound.

(3) The cyclist must obey all road signs, police signals, and traffic lights.

(4) Cyclists at night must show a bright white light to the front, and a red light and a red reflector at the back of the cycle. Red light and reflector may be incorporated.

There are lighting regulations which clearly define the performance of the rear light and reflector, and the position in which they must be fitted, as well as the size required. Your local Road Safety Officer can advise you on these regulations.

The Royal Society for the Prevention of Accidents (R.o.S.P.A.) produce a useful brochure on cycling technique and roadcraft called 'Skilful Cycling', it also includes signs, signals and road markings.

Code of the Countryside

These six rules seem basic enough, but it is helpful to list them, for they protect our countryside and safeguard the livelihood of farmers and livestock.

(1) Do not cause a fire. Never throw away lighted cigarette ends or lighted matches. Put out picnic fires with particular care, checking that they are completely out and won't flare up again later.

(2) Gates. If you open a gate, close it again. If you see a gate that has been left open, close that too. One straying animal can cause hundreds of pounds' worth of damage.

(3) Keep to the path. Grass as well as wheat is a crop. Do not walk or cycle through any crop.

(4) Litter. Valuable animals can die from eating plastic bags left by visitors or be injured by broken glass. Keep the cyclists' good reputation by taking litter home, or put it in the nearest litter bin in town or village.

(5) Keep water clean. Don't wash dishes (or yourself) in, or pollute in any way, water which may be used for farm purposes or as drinking water for animals.

(6) Protect wildlife and plants.

The Cotswold Past

To most people 'the past' may perhaps go back in their minds as far as Tudor times. Even the Saxon years seem so immensely long ago as to appear quite unreal. But to enjoy the Cotswolds there is a certain fascination in seeing the country in its historical context, and we are giving some very brief facts which may help to do this.

There *is* evidence that men lived in the Cotswolds 300,000 years before Christ – hand axes were found in the Evenlode Valley. But that's so infinitely distant that it is like thinking about the furthest stars. New people did come in 10,000 BC – lake-dwelling Scandinavians – and in 3,000 BC the people who lived in the Cotswolds actually had ideas about agriculture and keeping cattle. It was about then that a form of trade began to blossom all over Britain. People we call the 'Beaker Folk' (named, of course, after a distinctive beaker of theirs that was found) came to Britain in 2,000 BC. They knew how to work bronze and gold. The Cotswolds, then, were crossed for the first time by an important trade route from the centre of the Thames Valley to the routes in the north-west. All the trade routes were high – safe away from forests, wild beasts and enemies.

In 500 BC the Cotswolds were controlled by a fiery race called the Dubonni, who fought rival tribes to keep their Cotswold land, and who seem to have been based around Bagendon and North Cerney. There are traces of their fortified towns there, and terraces where they grew crops. When the Romans came to Britain, the Dubonni joined them to fight – and conquer – other rival tribes.

Rome in the Cotswolds

The Cotswolds missed the great Roman military pushes, when the legions marched across the country to the west, and from London towards Chester. The Romans made the centre where they lived in the Cotswolds at Cirencester – which they called Corinium. It seems they used the Cotswolds as a sort of holiday playground. This is believed because of the large number of Roman villas in the Cotswolds, for example Withington (it appears to have been lived-in *after* the Romans left), Chedworth with its hypocaust system of baths, Woodchester with its vast mosaic, and Ditchley which seems to have been a villa of two storeys.

The Romans grew corn in the Cotswolds. They needed huge quantities for their armies. For the first two or three hundred years of Roman rule it was the Cotswold corn that the Romans needed. Then came a move ... the first real move ... towards keeping sheep for their wool.

Vikings and Saxons

The Roman legions left. And for 400 years followed what are called the Dark Ages. England was in ferment. The land was invaded by Angles, Saxons, Jutes from Germany. Great bitter battles were fought with the native Romano-Britains and the Celts, who'd lived under Rome for so long. The Cotswolds were very much a border country, and Saxons, or Mercians, continued to raid the area, hungry to capture more land.

Then the Vikings came. They were from Denmark, and they were determined to conquer Britain instead of merely raiding it. They did conquer parts of the north and west of the country, and King Alfred was beaten twice and forced to pay the Vikings off. But he was a determined, shrewd and courageous leader, as well as a pious man and loved by his people, and when the Vikings came back for more he eventually defeated them, besieging their base camp at Chippenham and forcing them, finally, to accept peace.

In the Cotswolds there are still signs of the way Alfred then kept guard. He organised a number of country-wide danger signals, a series of beacons on the hilltops. If there was ever a sign of Vikings the fires were lit in a chain, from hill to hill, one after the other, and the people had time to fly, with wives, children, animals and goods, into fortified stockades.

Medieval Times

The Normans came, and England changed and settled. As the years went by, the woollen industry, which made the Cotswold villages, manors and churches which you see today, began to be famous all over Europe. Nearly all the villages became very rich. You can see this by the amazing number of those handsome, often elaborate churches called after the wool which paid for them. But the great rich days of the wool monopoly ended curiously. Edward IV, that brave, independent king who nevertheless wasn't very farsighted, gave the King of Spain two Cotswold rams as a present. And when these were cross-bred with the Spanish merinos, Spain produced wool of as good quality as that of the Cotswolds. It was a bitter blow. But wool remained very important up until the Industrial Revolution. And even today Witney blankets are said to be the finest in the world.

Finding History
You can see signs of this varied, sometimes violent history, in the Cotswolds still. The Rollright Stones which stand like petrified human creatures, were put there in 1500 B.C. by people who lived in the Cotswolds and who knew how to work in bronze and gold. At Chedworth's wonderful Villa there are moving signs of the kind of life the Romano-Britons lived, an elegant, civilised life in decorated, heated houses. And a wolf's head, guessed to have been carved by Vikings, snarls at the base of a door in Deerhurst's ancient church.

And for the rest – the whole country itself shows you, village after village, signs of its wool-trading centuries.

You can cover thousands of years of history in a few miles – if you know where to look. . . .

By the River Leach

Main centres and tours

Broadway

Perhaps this town, which used to be a little Cotswold village dependent upon sheep farming, is almost too famous, with its exquisite sweep of limestone buildings which make up the High Street. Broadway's anachronistic beauty has, to some extent, damaged it, for tourists come here in crowds, and the shops and cafés and places for souvenirs tend to destroy the atmosphere, however discreetly they're fitted into the façade. But there are still many beautiful places to look at, especially round the typical village green and along the High Street. The Lygon Arms is a seventeenth-century building, and the Tudor Horse is also worth visiting. And if you're interested in brasses, there's a fine one (a palimpsest, engraved on both sides) in Broadway's Norman church.

The most dramatic physical feature here at Broadway is the high bulk of Fish Hill, 1,024 feet, which dominates the town. The road from Broadway climbs more than 700 feet up in great sweeping curves. For the cyclist, a long pull – a push, mostly. But the views of the valleys of the Avon and the Severn really are marvellous when you get to the top of the hill. Here you'll see the strange little 'Fish Inn' which was originally a summer house. And not far from this is Broadway Tower, a folly built in 1800 by the Earl of Coventry, who wanted his wife to see thirteen counties at once! It needs pretty exceptional weather for the Earl's plan to come off, but the view *is* very beautiful. Look out for the famous Cross Hands signpost, one of the oldest in existence. It stands on the site of· a former gibbet where in 1661 three people were hanged for crimes they didn't commit. As you stand at the top of the hill, with the marvellous views all round you, that tragedy seems as far ago as Caesar.

Tours from Broadway

Broadway Tour One

Total distance: 15 miles.
O.S. Map: 144

Outward Route

Leave Broadway on the road for **Childs Wickham** (a right turn off the
A46, Cheltenham direction). Continue on this unclassified road to
Hinton on the Green and, at the next T junction, turn right and
cycle along the side of **Haseler Hill**. Haseler Hill is on the left with
sloping woods and on your right is **Merry Brook**. Turn right on to
the A44 into **Evesham**.

Homeward Route

Leave Evesham on the A44 in **Bretforton** direction, turning right
after two miles for **Badsey** down an unclassified road, running
parallel to the stream on your right (Badsey brook). Cycle through
Wickhamford, then turn left back into the main road A44 to return
to Broadway, passing through **Whitechapel** on your way.

Childs Wickham. The country here is rich with market gardens
and we saw many appetising notices: 'Honey and Apples, local
grown', 'Asparagus', 'Cherries', and 'Brown Eggs'. The lane runs
between high hedges, and the spire of the Norman church kept
disappearing as we went towards the village, lost by a turn in the
road or a cluster of trees. There are small cottages and a post office
of Cotswold stone. Look out for Childswickham House, a small
manor covered with clematis and roses in summer. If you have time,
visit the churchyard and see if you can find Mary Lane's grave. She
is supposed to have lived to be 133. We ourselves didn't find her
grave but it's worth searching.

Hinton on the Green. You cycle up to this village by an avenue of
trees, and we saw a Yucca flowering in a cottage opposite the church.
Yuccas are exotic plants and the flowers are heavy and cream-
coloured, with lily-like spires and sword leaves; they originated in
South America. We wanted to find William Halford's 600-year-old

monument in the church. We'd heard it was made of alabaster, showed Halford in his monk's robes, and must have been buried at some time since it was found in the churchyard, with the abbot's face downwards. But alas, the church was locked and a little notice said that it was 'void and destitute of a Pastor'. Gargoyles looked knowingly down at us, as if pleased that we couldn't get into the church. Opposite was an old house, very trim with well-kept lawns, and not far away we saw a handsome Tudor gatehouse with remains of towers on either side. This was once a great manor, burned in the Civil War.

The Civil War marked England inevitably. Across the Cotswolds you still find ruined mansions, the stains of flames or hollow of cannon shot on church walls. And it marked the people too. John Aubrey's vivid description tells how they looked:

'When the civil warres brake-out ... Mr. Hollar went into the Lowe Countries, where he stayed till about 1649. I remember he told me that when he first came into England, (which was a serene time of peace) that the people, both poore and rich, did looke cheerfully, but at his returne, he found the countenances of the people all changed, melancholy, spightfull, as if bewitched.'

Evesham. This town is also covered in our Broadway Week-End Tour. It's a town to linger in. Visit the Crown Hotel which is very ancient and has the kind of open courtyard used in medieval times by actors for their plays. There are tiny overlooking windows and you can imagine brightly-dressed people hundreds of years ago crowding to watch the players. We stopped by a useful black and gold notice in front of the timbered Medieval Almonry, which details the historic features of this marvellous market town. There are two churches, a Perpendicular bell tower and a timbered Abbey gatehouse all clustered together, with beautifully laid-out gardens down to the river in the background. On the side of the timbered gatehouse we saw the head of a girl, carved in stone with long flowing, very modern hair; the sculpture must have been 500 years old.

All Saints church is much restored but was built in the fourteenth century and has the beautiful St Clement's Chantry with its exquisite Tudor roof, fan-vaulted and carved in elaborate swirling patterns.

We were fascinated to see that the local workingmen's club has a doorway, topped by an ancient stone face, which was certainly once part of a church. It was a door much earlier than that of Tudor times. Simon de Montfort, who founded Parliament as we know it, was killed at the Battle of Evesham in 1265 and was buried under the high altar of the Abbey which vanished long ago.

Famous for its history, Evesham also has some very attractive and unusual shops. The 'Bird Cage' has a window full of handmade Cotswold treasures including speckled coffee-coloured pottery, rag dolls, necklaces and silver rings. There are a number of antique shops and the fruit and vegetable shops are full of delicious fresh local-grown produce.

Badsey. To reach Badsey you cycle through the fertile Vale of Evesham, along winding lanes, passing fields full of runner beans, asparagus fern, orchards, and one whole field of cultivated mauve scabious, the only one we saw and very beautiful. As you approach the village you pass Victorian and Edwardian villas which line the road, but turn sharp left to find the real Badsey. The manor house is exquisitely timbered with an overhanging roof and was built by the Hoby family. It's good to see that it is lived in, a real home still. The Midland Bank is a stone house 300 years old, and the church, St James's, with its blue clock, has well preserved and grotesque gargoyles. Facing the cosy *Wheat Sheaf Inn* is a big Cromwellian stone house.

Whickhamford. The country is flat and easy for cycling, and the village takes some finding. It is down among the orchards near Badsey Brook. There's been a lot of new development round here, which often means that new roads intersect with old ones, and the village is inclined to disappear! Near the water is a Tudor house facing a lake; the famous Sandys family lived here. If you have time, visit the church to look at their memorials. There are alabaster tombs of the Sandys, including Jacobeans with wives and children. How often in these memorials you'll see little carved statues of tiny babies. We suppose these were the infants who died at birth – there's something very touching about these tiny sculpted figures in their swaddling clothes and bonnets. Incidentally, one of this family, Sir Edwyn (you'll see his figure in a memorial with his eight children) married Penelope Washington, an ancestress of George Washington's.

Broadway Tour Two (Round Bredon Hill)

Total distance: 29 miles.
O.S. Map: 144.

Outward Route

Take the Cheltenham road (A46) out of Broadway, turning right in about 1½ miles for **Dumbleton**, following the same road until you meet the A435. Turn left into the A435 for one mile, until the next crossroad, then turn right to **Beckford**. Cycle through Beckford for **Conderton** and **Overbury** and **Kemerton**. Keep straight ahead at the three-road junction, and turn right when you join B4080 for **Eckington**. After visiting the village, cycle on the same road until it joins the A440 turning right for **Pershore**.

Homeward Route

Take the A44 out of Pershore in the Evesham direction, branching right, and right again on to unclassified road for **Great Comberton** and **Little Comberton**. Turn right for **Bricklehampton** and **Elmley Castle**. Take left fork for **Netherton** and **Hinton on the Green**, crossing the A435 and returning through **Childs Wickham** to Broadway.

Beckford. The village stands on the site of a Romano-British settlement and was mentioned in Domesday Book. Beckford Hall, among high trees, was a Catholic stronghold from troubled religious times until the end of the last century. In the 1930s it was bought by the Salesian Fathers for their students. There's a strong tradition that a passage leads from the ancient priory crypt (which was part of the manor and dates from the 1300s) right under, the hills to Elmley Castle! We liked the golden stone church with its black clock and arched windows. The earliest part is twelfth-century. On the lower side of the village the river Currant winds through apple and pear orchards. Some of these are no longer producing fruit but are used for mistletoe which grows on the ancient trunks and is sold at Christmastime.

Conderton. There's an interesting old pub, called the Yew Tree Inn, named after a huge yew which stands on the corner like a vast pointed umbrella. If you're interested in Roman history there was once a Roman village and a settlement near here. To reach the site, take the road up through the centre of the village and follow it for half a mile. Here the road bends sharply to the left and becomes a track which runs beside a wood. Further on you'll find a rectangular earthwork, about two and a half acres. The Roman village was sheltered here, and water was close by.

Overbury. People say it is one of the best-kept villages in Worcestershire. The houses are beautifully looked-after, built in Cotswold stone with climbing roses, little gardens and grassy verges. A stream runs down the side of the churchyard and fills a pool nearby.

We saw Overbury Court standing among high cedars behind grey walls. The whole village is owned by the Overbury Estate which is why it is so cared for. We were curious about a tomb set right in the middle of the lychgateway to the church and wondered why this important site should have been chosen. Perhaps to ask the villagers for a prayer as they went into church. The church, which has a marvellous magnolia tree, is dedicated to St Faith, whose relics were brought to this country in Saxon times.

Kemerton. Another enchanting village with flower-covered garden walls, a straggling little place on the south of Bredon Hill. Standing on the heights above Kemerton is an odd building called Bell's Castle. If you have time you might like to climb up to have a closer look. It was built in 1825 by a sailor called Bell from the Isle of Wight and was originally two Jacobean cottages, altered and extended into a castle by Bell, with battlements and a look-out post. It's believed locally that Bell was a kind of pirate attacking French ships during the post-Waterloo years and storing his booty in his castle. In the village the Crown Hotel looked attractive but we didn't have time to stop on our journey.

Eckington. As you cycle to this village you will see Bredon Hill in the distance, a rounded misty shape. Housman's poem in which the lovers lie on the top of Bredon Hill and 'see the coloured counties and hear the larks so high' has made this hill immortal. Eckington Bridge, built in the 1500s, crosses the Avon and barges slip by, as they've been doing since the bridge was built, although the waterway was infinitely more busy then. The greatest treasure in the village is the cross in a small memorial garden near the crossroads. It was used as a preaching cross by the monks who lived at Pershore Abbey but its top was added in Victorian times. The village is fair-sized and you'll see black and white houses and little cottages. But cycle off the main road to find the prettiest and quaintest corners. The road, the B4080, which passes the village, is a straight, good and fast cycling road.

Pershore. This is a busy small market town which has the remains of a marvellous Abbey – one of the largest that existed in the Midlands. Pershore's Abbey is set among lawns and high trees and was once enormous . . . over a hundred yards in length. Despite the fact that it was partly destroyed by Henry VIII at the time of the dissolution of the monasteries, it's still a noble building. The battlements and flying buttresses are fourteenth century, the lantern tower has pinnacles and turrets. You'll see some ancient stained glass which tells the story of the town, including the Vikings destroying the monastery in Saxon times, Edward the Confessor, Queen Elizabeth on her way to visit Elmley Castle, and folk dancing round the maypole at the churchyard fair. Pershore is a well-kept, elegant place with Regency balconies and attractive antique shops. We had excellent toasted sandwiches and luscious local cider at the Royal Three Tuns; the hotel is close to the Abbey and it's inexpensive and friendly.

Great Comberton. As you cycle up to the village you will see the square tower of the church, St Michael and All Angels, which has choir stalls of Jacobean carved panelling; the benches are sixteenth-century, plain and massive. The parish, incidentally, once belonged to Henry VIII's last queen, Katherine Parr, who lived the last years of her life at Sudeley Castle near Winchcombe. Look across the field from the church, beside the main road, and you'll see a beautiful black and white timbered house, believed to have been the fourteenth-century Rectory. The road through Great Comberton winds through orchards and wheatfields.

Little Comberton. The pleasant lonely road is a perfect one for the cyclist, under tall grey aspen trees. There's a sharp turn in the road by the church, under some high cedars. There are many delightful timbered cottages; one of them has an overhanging timber-framed gable. Opposite the church is a timbered-framed house known as The Old House, built in the sixteenth century; a little distance away is Nash's Farm, another sixteenth-century timbered house with a great circular pigeon house with 684 holes for the birds.

Your return journey after Little Comberton takes you through **Elmley Castle, Netherton, Hinton on the Green** and **Childs Wickham** back to **Broadway.** If you wish to spend a little extra time in any of these places, there are full details of them in the Broadway Week-End cycle tour in this book.

Broadway Tour Three

Total distance: 17 miles
O.S. Map: 144

Outward Route

Take the unclassified road due south to **Snowshill**. Continue cycling through Snowshill until you reach a T junction. Turn right on to unclassified road, cycle four miles until you meet the crossroads linking with B4077. Turn right for **Ford** and **Stanway**.

Homeward Route

Leave Stanway on B4077 for **Toddington**, crossing the A46 on to the A438, from which you turn right into Toddington village. Cycle through village and turn left on to the A46, back to Broadway.

Snowshill. Here is a magnificent Tudor manor with a south front of about 1700, and one of the most interesting and beautiful places to visit near Broadway. King Henry VIII gave the house to Katherine Parr as part of her dowry, but later when he died and she married Thomas Seymour, who was executed for treason, the manor reverted to the Royal family.

Snowshill Manor and its gardens are National Trust property and are open, during May to September, on Wednesdays, Thursdays, Saturdays, Sundays and Bank Holidays, from 11 to 1, and from 2 to 6. The gardens are terraced and decorated, designed as a series of cottage gardens, with flowering rockeries, stone walls, old roses, other old-fashioned flowers and clipped yews. The house stands among high trees and is a real gem. The most fascinating thing is the 'Magpie Museum' which Mr Charles Wade, a scholar, architect and artist-craftsman, collected together and presented to the National Trust. He bought Snowshill Manor in 1919 when it was a farmhouse in a bad state of repair and spent the rest of his life until he died in 1956, restoring the house and collecting together his 'magpie' treasures. Cyclists will be particularly interested in 'The Great Garret or 100 Wheels' which has many early bicycles, including the Hobby Horse, 1790, and a cycle from Norfolk with a wooden frame, forks and wheels, as well as other wooden-wheeled bikes (the prototypes of the penny-farthing). There are also coaches, sedan chairs, chariots,

Snowshill Manor

Yarmouth herring carts, and a model of the State palanquin of a Maharajah. In other rooms are magnificent collections of musical instruments, armour (including elaborate Japanese armour), lace-making exhibits, and many other fascinating items of every kind.

Stanway. The road to Stanway takes you through a country of magnificent trees, with a little stream running in the valley. The village is in a dip and can be seen among its wooded hills, the buildings clustered close. Stanway House, the gateway of which is right in the middle of the village, is stunning, built next to the church. Both are of golden stone and quite perfect. The gate – probably designed by Inigo Jones – is decorated with a coat of arms, and repeated patterns of scallop shells on the tops of the gables. And through this elaborate gatehouse you can glimpse Stanway House, a seventeenth-century hall. We couldn't see the tulip tree on the lawn under which Edward VII had tea when a thunderstorm broke up the royal party!

The village has a tithe barn which was mentioned in Domesday Book. Stanway is too beautiful not to visit when you are cycling through the Cotswolds.

Toddington. The narrow lane to the village is literally enclosed by woods, the daylight almost excluded by dark trees. A little notice says: 'To church and village hall.' It's a lonely place, and when we went into the church it was almost eerie to see the tomb of the Traceys, Charles Henbury Tracey, first Baron Sudeley and his wife Henrietta. They built the neighbouring manor house in 1829. Their life-sized figures lie together in marble, wearing formal solemn draperies, he in peer's robes and she in a flowing embroidered dress. Henrietta, we thought, looked very ill and wasted and this gave a gloomy feeling to the chapel where they lie so still.

The Traceys have always been both famous and infamous in this part of the country because of their connexion with the murder of Thomas à Beckett. We noticed, over and over again, how this murder has been on the Cotswold conscience. We've seen stained glass windows showing the deed, and many, many churches dedicated to the murdered saint. We were therefore particularly interested to find the ruins of a seventeenth-century manor nearby where the Traceys used to live. All we could find, finally, as we peered through a thick overgrown screen of trees and hedges, was the outline of a ruined manor gatehouse, with its arching gateway, carved coat of arms against the wilderness, and some other ruins all overgrown with brambles. It was melancholy, but do see it if you can find it.

Stanway House

Broadway Tour Four

Outward Route

Climb Fish Hill out of Broadway (it is rather steep but the rest of the ride is worth it). Turn right at the top of the hill on to unclassified road running due south for **Snowshill**. Turn left at next crossroad and cycle through **Toddington** and **Cutsdean**, still on unclassified roads (about three miles). Then turn left and almost immediately right for **Temple Guiting**. After visiting Temple Guiting, turn right on to unclassified road, passing Guiting wood on the right. After three miles, turn right on to the Salt Way (old Roman Road), following the outer park wall of Sudeley Castle to **Winchcombe**.

Homeward Route

After visiting Winchcombe, cycle along the A46 (Broadway direction) for two miles, then turn right for **Hailes Abbey**. After visiting the Abbey return to the A46 and continue in the Broadway direction for three miles, turning right on to unclassified road to **Stanton**. Cycle through the village to rejoin the A46 back to Broadway.

Temple Guiting. The village is in the valley of the Windrush river which flows under beach trees. The church is small and has some ancient stained glass which is interesting – 15th century glass showing St Mary Magdalene, St James and the Virgin Mary. Just behind the church is a little pond and beyond it an enchanting stone house, mullion-windowed, overlooking the river. The house, at the top of a grassy bank, is where the Bishops of Oxford used to spend their summers. We understand why, as it was enchanting. As you cross the river you'll see other Tudor stone houses on the river banks.

Winchcombe. There are hills all round this lovely town and the winding street is edged with ancient houses and rather alluring shops. Facing the church is a magnificent Jacobean house, and further down the street is the galleried George Inn and another old inn with the amusing name of *The Corner Cupboard*. If you have time, don't miss Sudeley Castle which we thought was the best small castle we've ever visited. Katherine Parr lived and died here and her tomb can be seen in the private chapel in the castle gardens. In what remains of the castle are marvellous treasures including letters from Katherine, a lock of her hair and a miniature of her with Thomas Seymour, the attractive, dangerous man she married after Henry died. For students of Tudor history, Sudeley has everything – its past is tragic, its setting beautiful and serene, its atmosphere harmonious. In the town of Winchcombe, visit the church where you'll see a number of famous grotesques, and a piece of embroidery by Queen Katherine of Aragon. There is also a folk museum in the Town Hall with a number of interesting locally-found treasures.

Hailes Abbey. There's very little left of what was once a vast Cistercian abbey of the 13th century. It was here that King Henry III came with his queen and hundreds of knights and bishops to attend the consecration of thirteen abbey altars. Henry was deeply pious – he was also rather weak and artistic – and when he visited King Louis in France he called at so many churches to pray on his way to the royal meeting that he never arrived that day! King Louis (who, incidentally, is *Saint* Louis) wisely closed the churches next time so that Henry and he could actually meet and talk.

You'll need imagination, at Hailes, to re-create that pious, weak king among these peaceful stones. There are a number of arches still standing – part of the cloisters where the monks walked and said their daily office. The arches at least will give you a faint idea of the beauty of the abbey, destroyed at the Reformation. The ruins today are so well cared for by the National Trust, with soft green lawns between arches and gateways, it's odd to think that as recently as the 1900s grass, trees and brambles covered the whole of Hailes Abbey, growing over six feet high. The abbey is open from March to October, 9.30 to 5, Sundays 2 to 7. In the winter months it opens from 9.30 to 4. There is a small museum next to the abbey, which has early tiles, bosses and other relics rescued from the ruins. The little church facing the abbey is partly Norman, with a thirteenth-century arch, and you'll see some panels of glass which actually came from the abbey, with figures of saints.

Stanton. Very close to the village of Stanway, with a similar-sounding name, Stanton is a twin in beauty with a series of lovely houses, one of which has '1618' over its doorway. The village is built on a gentle hill with gardens and small lawns climbing up to a larch wood. There are beautiful views in the distance and we saw a wealth of Hidcote blue lavender. There are thatched barns in the village and several old manor houses, including Stanton Court which was built in Tudor times.

29   *Hailes Abbey*

Burford

Like so many others in the Cotswolds, Burford is an old wool town built around one handsome main High Street. The town is on the side of a hill, leading from the Oxford–Cheltenham road down to the Windrush valley. There are many varied kinds of building in its graceful sweep, but the overall impression is still of that instantly recognisable, warm, honey-coloured Cotswold stone.

Burford church is large – the second biggest in Oxfordshire, with a beautiful tall spire; it has memories of the Civil War. In 1649 some mutineers were trapped there in the church, and three of them were later shot. There is supposed to be a bullet scar still on the church wall.

The town attracts a lot of visitors. You'll understand this when you look round at the many finely preserved old houses. There's the Methodist chapel which was converted from a Georgian town house, the Bull Inn, the Mermaid, the Old Lamb, the sixteenth-century Crown, and many others. Opposite the Bull is a private house which used to be another inn. The rakish George IV stayed there when he came to Bibury races.

Burford has a tradition of building. Three of Christopher Wren's master masons were Burford men; the reason is probably because of the marvellous quality of Burford stone. When Wren was designing St Paul's, he insisted on Burford stone for certain parts of his cathedral.

Tours from Burford

Burford Tour One

Total distance: 19 miles.
O.S. Map: 144.

Outward Route

Leave Burford on the A424, heading towards Stow-on-the-Wold, but turning left on to unclassified road as soon as you have crossed the river Windrush. Continue cycling through **Taynton** to **Great Barrington** (approximately three miles). Site of Roman building on left as you turn right for **Great Rissington**, still on unclassified roads. Cycle due north for approximately 2½ miles, then turn left into Great Rissington. Continue cycling by this road up to **Bourton-on-the-Water**.

Homeward Route

Leaving Bourton, take unclassified road in a southerly direction to **Sherborne**, passing alongside Sherborne Park and crossing the Sherborne brook. Continue cycling on same road to **Windrush** which takes its name from the river. Cycle through Windrush, turning left for **Little Barrington** and turning left again to cycle alongside the river Windrush back to Burford, all the way on unclassified roads.

Great Barrington. The Windrush flows by under two little bridges, and if you want to find the church cycle across the river and up a winding hill, turning left at the top into the church lane.

As in many Cotswold villages, the church and a great house stand side by side. In this case the house seemed to us deserted – certainly the wing close to the church was empty and covered with yellow roses. Down the side of the churchyard is a sunny wall against which a stone seat has been set. It would seat at least ten people. One could imagine the village elders sunning themselves here, probably disapproving of the flighty young ones on Sundays.

We visited the church because we were fascinated by the legend of Captain Bray who is buried here. When Queen Elizabeth forgave him for killing a man, he swore he would never use his right hand on his sword again. Sure enough, on his tomb we saw that his sword is on the wrong side.

Sherborne is a straggling village of stone houses winding up and down leafy lanes. The Sherborne brook is nearby and there is a waterfall in the great deer park. Perhaps the most amusing thing to look for is a cottage which was once a thirteenth-century church. It is No. 88, the last cottage on the Windrush road. There are marvellous Celtic crosses and zigzag patterns over and around the small front door, and there are two other Norman doorways. It is most strange to see a church entrance on an ordinary lived-in house with curtains at the windows.

Over the doorway of No. 44, also in Sherborne, we saw another fragment of history. This was a solemn Norman face carved in stone and wearing a helmet. He now sprouts flowers, but he must have been a hero, once upon a time.

Windrush. The village is named after the famous river which flows down the valley, and eventually joins the Thames. The church faces a small triangular patch of green, with big elm trees round it. Anybody exploring the Cotswolds must sooner or later become engrossed with the extraordinary decoration in stone in the shape of birds' heads, called 'beak-heads'. This is a Norman style of decoration, and the beak-heads alter from church to church. They are rather like slit-eyed, mischievous looking owls or eagles. Beaks can be long or short, according to the whim of the sculptor. On the Windrush church the beak-heads are in very good condition, there's a double row of them, deeply carved. Some of the beaks seem to wear formal curly beards. We wondered if these were the male beaks, and the others their ladies.

Little Barrington. This gorgeous village is on either side of a miniature stream in what must have been the river bed, now overgrown. The ducks seem to be sailing on grass, for the stream is so narrow and the grass banks so lush. Visit the tiny church, syringa bushes surround it and smell marvellous in summertime. And on the right side of the porch as you enter the churchyard (hidden by the porch itself until you actually walk round the side) is a fascinating carving. It's a monument to William Taylor, 1669, but there are four figures believed to be much older; two little girls in bonnets and capes, holding hands, and two boys in long coats, hatless. All four figures are innocent and charming.

Bourton-on-the-Water. This village, with its bridges and river, its old houses and willows, is fully covered in our cycling tour planned for a weekend based on Moreton-in-the-Marsh.

Burford Tour Two

Total distance: 16 miles.
O.S. Maps 144/157

Outward Route

Leave Burford on the A433 (Bibury direction). Half a mile beyond **Aldsworth** turn left on to unclassified road for **Coln St Aldwyns** and **Hatherop**. Turn left out of Hatherop for **Eastleach Turville** and **Eastleach Martin,** turning right along the east bank of the river Leach, cycling to **Southrop**.

Homeward Route

Retrace for $\frac{1}{4}$ mile on the Southrop road and then turn right for **Filkins**. Again, retrace your track for $\frac{1}{2}$ mile to return by the unclassified road to **Westwell**; after about three miles, turn right into the village of Westwell, and continue by same road back to Burford.

Aldsworth. Round this village, browsing in the fields, you may see some flocks of the original breed of Cotswold sheep, whose wool made the whole area famous. The ancient church has an unusual gallery outside the west end – with a flight of stone steps leading up to it. And one of the windows has small fragments of old stained glass, bordered by crowns and roses.

Coln St Aldwyn. It's odd to cycle into this quiet little farming village and consider that a Chancellor of the Exchequer in Queen Victoria's reign lived here, it seems so far removed from the world of finance. He was the first Earl St Aldwyn, and we peeped through the gateway leading to the impressive grey manor house, with a big coat of arms over the doorway. We suppose he lived here – it is certainly grand enough.

The route from Coln St Aldwyn to Hatherop takes you through beautiful parkland, with a river running through rich pastures and cattle grazing everywhere. Hatherop, where they make weather vanes at a tiny ironworks, has a magnificent manor on the right as you cycle by.

The East Leaches. They are twin Cotswold villages, Eastleach Martin and Eastleach Turville, divided by the river Leach. As we came towards them we saw a hare with black-tipped ears, who galloped in front of us for several yards and finally hopped over a stone wall.

There are copses in the distance, hedges for birds to nest in, and little cottages with gardens in summer full of catmint and valerian. The tiny church in an overgrown field once had five sundials, to represent five brothers who died fighting for William the Conqueror. Alas, we could find no trace of the sundials now. But we did hear something mournful and strange – it was the cry of a peacock echoing through the village, doubtless from a manor house nearby.

Southrop. You cycle past two magnificent manor houses, there's a stream rippling by, and flowers sprout from stone walls everywhere. Clipped yew hedges give a Tudor look to this small village full of country pursuits. We saw many young children trotting by on ponies. Visit the church and look at the font, twelfth-century, with the deeply carved figures of virtues stamping on fat, rather humble vices. On the altar are two marvellous Tudors, a girl in her Paris veil, the man in armour, his hair in the 1970's style, his head on his helmet. They are life-sized and beautifully preserved. There is an extremely pleasant-looking pub, *The Swan*, at Southrop, which looked just right for a cyclist's stop.

Filkins. We wanted to trace this name, surely it has some magical or rustic significance. But no one seems to know its origin. If you didn't linger in Southrop you may like to stop for a while at the *Lamb Inn* here, it is ivy-covered and looks most pleasant and welcoming. We saw a rare shrub, a climbing laburnum, growing against a wall and covered in flowers, and there seemed to be plentiful wild flowers growing outside every cottage. In a miniature ex-Nonconformist chapel is probably the smallest country museum in England. It's here that you can see relics of yesterday, old horse and oxen shoes, threshing implements, Roman coins dug up in the fields nearby, seventeenth-century trade tokens, and many other small treasures of country life. But the museum was locked the day we were there, so we peeped in through the window and saw a Victorian wheel chair as well as the farm implements on walls and shelves. You must contact George Swinford next to the Vicarage if you want to browse around yourself.

Southrop

Burford Tour Three

Total distance: 28 miles.
O.S. Maps: 144/157.

Outward Route

Leave Burford in a southerly direction (crossing the A40 Northleach to Witney road) and take the unclassified road to **Westwell**, continuing through Westwell on the same road for further three miles, before forking left for **Eastleach Turville**. Cycle on same road for three miles, passing disused airfield on left, then turn left into **Fairford**. Take main road out of Fairford for **Lechlade**, A417, cycle four miles to Lechlade.

Homeward Route

Turn left out of Lechlade in northerly direction on A361 for **Little Faringdon**. Here turn right on to unclassified road for **Langford** and **Broadwell**, and **Kencot**. Continue cycling on this road for further 2½ miles until it rejoins the A361, turning right for Signet and Burford.

Fairford. This market town on the river Coln is very pleasant, and you'll enjoy lingering here for a while, it has real Cotswold atmosphere. Many of the buildings are of stone or timbered, and there's a charming old stone house which was once a free school standing facing the church. It was founded by Richard Green, who died in 1767, and is now a youth centre.

Fairford church is rightly famous for its marvellous stained glass windows, mostly fifteenth and sixteenth century; it's believed the windows are of the school of Barnard Flower, Master Glass Painter to King Henry VII. One of the remarkable things about this stained glass is the freshness of many green tones, used for trees, streams, Thames landscapes, lakes and grasses. The subjects are always holy (Moses, Gideon, King Solomon, the Three Kings) but the settings are endearingly local. But tear your eyes away from the windows to look at the carvings on the choir stalls, also of Henry VII's time. They are so alive and vivid, and very funny. There's a young man teasing a girl, a wife beating her husband, women plucking a pigeon, and a couple draining a cider barrel. Here's Cotswold life nearly 500 years ago.

On the outskirts of Fairford we saw a most attractive restaurant, a series of white-painted cottages with the odd name of *Pinks*. We heard that it is run by ladies, and that the dining-room has a stone floor and a beamed ceiling. Pinks offers you French or English cooking. We didn't feel rich enough to try it out, but if you have cause for a celebration during this cycle trip, it would be fun to eat here.

Lechlade. The rivers Leach and Coln flow into the Thames just near the town, and a mile away three counties meet (Berkshire, Gloucestershire and Wiltshire). We crossed the old Halfpenny Bridge across the Thames. Long ago this town was well known for its great press of barge traffic, as many as a hundred barges jostling each other beside the bridges at one time. Some of these carried the stones which were used to build the dome of St Paul's Cathedral. On the A417 is a very pleasant old stone house, bow fronted, with a sundial over its doorway. By the old St John's Bridge, where the Leach joins the Thames, is the famous *Trout Inn*. It was an almshouse in the twelfth century and was granted, at that time, two miles of Thames fishing rights, held under Royal Charter. Trout is a speciality, and there's a good range of snacks, which you eat by an open fire on a chilly day, in a panelled and beamed bar.

Buscot Old Parsonage. If you are a real garden lover, it is well worth fixing a cycle trip on a Wednesday so that you can visit the Old Parsonage here. The house, and its lovely gardens, are open every Wednesday from two to six. But write in advance and arrange it. (The house lies two miles south-east of Lechlade and four miles north-west of Faringdon). You'll see beautiful grounds, with lakes, water-garden, a large kitchen garden and greenhouses.

Kencot. Some of the small Cotswold villages take a bit of finding. You really have to search for this one – and the church is even more tucked away, set back from a small, quiet road with an elm nearly twenty feet round facing it. The church is very small, with no towers at all, and looks quite bobbed!

We were very intrigued with a sign which we found over the church doorway – one of those mystifying signs of pagan feeling in an early Christian England which seemed to us to appear all over the Cotswolds. This time it was a Norman artist's work; he had carved a big figure of Sagittarius (and carved its title over it, obviously the sculptor was interested in horoscopes). The figure is a centaur, half man (with a Norman face and hair) and half horse. He's shooting an arrow into the mouth of a dragon large enough to have swallowed him whole. If you can sketch, this sculpture would make an interesting drawing.

Burford Tour Four

Total distance: 30 miles.
O.S. Maps: 144, 145, 157, 158.

Outward Route

Leave Burford on the A40 (Witney direction). Turn *sharp* left at White Hill on to unclassified road to **Widford** and **Swinbrook**. Cycle east to **Asthall Leigh** (still on unclassified road) then sharp right to **Minster Lovell**. Cycle through the village, cross the A40 and take unclassified road to **Brize Norton** and Bampton. Turn right on to A4095 to **Clanfield** then right on to B4449 (Lechlade direction). Just before Lechlade turn sharp left on A417 to **Buscot**.

Homeward Route

Cycle back from Buscot on A417 to **Lechlade**, then the A361 to **Filkins** and Burford.

Widford. To find the rare church you must turn left at the Mill Farm over a tiny bridge beside a spinney of poplars. You'll see a fine Elizabethan manor house on the hill. Cycle up to a gate which leads to a church right in the middle of sloping fields. The path is under elm trees and up a little slope – and there is the church. It was built by monks on the remains of a Roman Villa and founded in 1100; it is named after St Oswald whose body is said to have rested in this little lost place. The church has remains of real Roman mosaic pavements, whiteish and greenish. There's a wall painting of kings and a devil with his finger to his nose, surely a doom painting (its date is 1350); it shows 'three living and three dead – as we are, so you will be', a religious warning often used by the Church in those times.

From the church you can take a footpath with your bicycle, or ride by the little road to **Swinbrook** (also covered in Northleach Week-End Tour). This church is famous for its six reclining figures, three Elizabethans and three Stuarts, all members of the Fettiplace family. They're marvellous, and rather comical, somebody said they were like 'passengers on a Victorian steamer'. It's interesting to see the difference between the stiff Elizabethan gentlemen and the Stuarts, who looked more fleshly and pleasure-loving, wearing lace and ribbons. The Fettiplaces were a rich family for hundreds of years and married heiresses, too. But the family died out in the early nineteenth century and their beautiful house, said to be the finest Tudor manor in the country, was deserted, then pillaged, and then fell into ruins. Nothing is left but a little dairy with a Tudor roof by the church. The Jacobean brass chandeliers in the church, by the way, came from Lady Redesdale's ballroom – it's odd to think they once shone over dancers to waltzes. She was mother to the brilliant Mitford girls – Nancy who wrote 'The Pursuit of Love' and Jessica, authoress of 'Hons and Rebels'. Another sister was the stormy Unity who died, aged only 34, in 1948. She is buried here in the churchyard, and on her grave, of golden Cotswold stone already weathering, are the moving words: 'Say not the struggle naught availeth'. There are also memorials to the Mitfords' parents, Lord and Lady Redesdale, and to their only brother, killed in the last war in Burma. The Redesdale family used to live at Asthall Manor.

Minster Lovell (also covered in Northleach Week-End Tour). Don't miss a chance to look, perhaps for a second time, at these marvellous ruins of a late medieval manor, the home of the Lovells who fought with Richard III and lost the battle with him at Bosworth. William, Lord Lovell, who built this vast house – now only a few high walls and grassy courtyards – is buried in the church next to the ruins. He has a magnificent alabaster tomb with painted shields in scarlet and gold. And there's the extraordinary dovecote nearby, a circular tower with a tiled roof where the pigeons nested in boxes by the hundred. What an amazing noise that must have been when they were all there together!

Buscot Park. The house, which is open on Wednesdays and first Saturdays in the month from April to September, 2 to 6, and from October to March on Wednesdays only, is late eighteenth-century, in the Adam style, all elegance and formality. There are water gardens and a lovely park, 55 acres in extent. If you visit the house, you must see the 'Briar Rose' paintings by Burne Jones – the pre-Raphaelites have become so popular recently that there's a great revival of interest in this artist with his beautiful, dreamy women in glowing colours. There are also Rembrandts and others.

Filkins. (This village is also covered in Burford Tour Two.) It's only a tiny village but very charming and full of cottages and gardens, some with yews cut into shapes. The miniature museum with its relics of local country life is in the smallest house used as a museum that we've ever seen, a tiny place once a Nonconformist chapel.

Pump Room, Cheltenham

Cheltenham

The largest town in the area, Cheltenham has a race course (everybody knows the Cheltenham Gold Cup), and some famous music festivals. It's an amusing coincidence that Cheltenham was the birthplace of a famous jockey – Fred Archer – *and* a famous musician, Gustav Holst. And racing and music are part of its life.

It wasn't until the eighteenth century that the English aristocracy became aware of Cheltenham. The town is situated at the foot of the Cotswolds scarp-slope and is technically a spring-lime settlement. It was this which made Cheltenham's fortune. When the mineral springs were discovered, the little town became transformed in a few years into a Spa which was the height of fashion. Cobbett, in the early nineteenth century, disapprovingly called it a place to which 'gluttons, drunkards and debauchees of all descriptions resort . . . in the hope of getting rid of the bodily consequences of their manifold sins and iniquities.' Looking at the Regency houses, so very stylish, including a great promenade and fronted by lawns, which are now municipal offices, one can just imagine spoiled, painted Regency people, exquisitely dressed and eager for gossip, who made Cheltenham famous while they 'took the waters' hopefully for their health.

When you are in Cheltenham, don't miss the delightful Montpellier Rotunda, the Regency schools, and the art gallery.

Two miles south, at Leckhampton Hill, is the Devil's Chimney, an extraordinary pinnacle of rock at the top of a cliff, overlooking Cheltenham, like a huge stone creature rather than a chimney.

Tours from Cheltenham

Cheltenham Tour One

Total distance: 21 miles.
O.S. Map: 144.

Outward Route

Leave Cheltenham on the B4070 for Prestbury. After **Prestbury**, join the A46 for 1½ miles to **Southam**. Fork left at Southam on to unclassified road for **Woodmancote**, then right again for **Gotherington**. Half a mile beyond Gotherington turn left on to the B4079 for 2½ miles to **Pamington**. At Pamington turn left and take secondary road to join the A438 into Tewkesbury.

Homeward Route

Take the road out of **Tewkesbury** (due south) unclassified, cycling to **Tredington**; after one mile turn left into Stoke Orchard and continue two miles to **Bishops Cleeve**. Turn right at Bishops Cleeve on to A435 to Cheltenham.

Prestbury. The Roundheads were stationed here in the Civil War when the Cavaliers had their headquarters at Sudeley Castle. There are thatched and beamed houses in the village; some of these were eighteenth-century almshouses. In the past, almshouses belonged to monasteries, where alms and hospitality were given to visitors, but by the eighteenth century they had become houses built by charity for the 'aged poor'. It's interesting that almshouses are invariably simple but beautiful in style, and very homely.

Tewkesbury. The Severn and Avon rivers join here, and the Avon is spanned by King John's bridge which was built in 1200. The town has a number of attractive timbered houses and inns. We liked the

Plough, which has oak-beamed ceilings, bars with copper tables, and antique coaching lamps. Mr Pickwick visited Tewkesbury in Dickens' comic novel, and dined at the Hop Pole – rather well, it seemed, for he slept through the next thirty miles of his journey.

The most moving and impressive sight, of course, in Tewkesbury is the Abbey. It is magnificent, stately but not ponderous, a mixture of colours – gold, brown, cream and soft grey, and surrounded by fine and varied trees.

The Abbey was built by monks in the 1100s, and there is a gatehouse and Abbot's lodge, part of what was once a kind of small town of religious buildings. The Abbey itself is a masterpiece of Norman work. Among so many rich things to see, look at the fourteenth-century glass in the choir windows and you'll notice a particular shade of brilliant translucent green, a typical tint of the period, used by the stained glass artists.

The tomb of Richard of Worcester is in the Beauchamp chantry, the shields still boldly coloured. On the inner side of the sacristy door you will see metal strips strengthening it. These are thought to have been made from armour from the dead soldiers after the battle of Tewkesbury in 1471.

Half a mile south of Tewkesbury is the site of that battle, in the Wars of the Roses, when Queen Margaret was defeated and her son Edward, Prince of Wales, killed. In Shakespeare's histories, the Queen sees him murdered by Gloucester in front of her eyes and cries out: 'Oh Ned, sweet Ned, speak to thy mother, boy! . . .

> Butchers and villains! bloody cannibals!
> How sweet a plant have you untimely cropped! . . .'

It is one of the most tragic parts of·the play, whose bloody history takes place at Tewkesbury.

Bishop's Cleeve. The cottages are timbered and whitewashed, bright in summer with red geraniums. The Tithe Barn is a joy, it has now been turned into a most unusual school. It's good to see an ancient barn actually being used today for children rather than preserved as a piece of history. The church has fine cedars round it and a carved porch. Look on the outside of the church at the base of the tower at some little figures, a carving of a small man clutching an enormous stone (was he one of the masons who built the tower?) and a huge bird with a fat body and straddling legs. Much of Bishop's Cleeve is thatched. In the distance is a hill, 1,000 feet up, with the beautiful name of Cleeve Cloud.

Cheltenham Tour Two

Total distance: 21 miles.
O.S. Map: 144.

Outward Route

Take the A40 road out of Cheltenham in the Northleach direction, cycling through **Charlton Kings** and **Dowdeswell**, forking right, almost immediately, on to unclassified road for **Withington**.

Homeward Route

At Withington, turn right on to unclassified road for **Colesborne**, cycling through Colesborne Park alongside the river Hilcot Brook and turning right to join the A435. Cycle for ¾ mile, then turn left on to unclassified road through Colesborne. Half a mile later turn right at crossroads for **Cowley** (the hill is steep, Bubb's Hill on this route, but well worth the climb). (*Old Cross at Cowley*.) Cycle on unclassified road out of Cowley to **Ullenwood**, crossing the A436 and joining the B4070 back into **Cheltenham**.

Charlton Kings. The little church has a squat tower, and the attractive rose window has a crown in its centre. On the outside of the church, on corners and cornices, are some interesting carved faces, many of which looked to us like the stone portraits of craftsmen of the past. One curious thing in the church is a window in memory of Robert Podmore which was placed there by officers of the Imperial Japanese Navy in 1906. It's believed to be the first instance of the Japanese nation honouring somebody British. Robert served with them in gun trials in a ship called 'Katori'.

Dowdeswell. Cycling along the A40 there is a marvellous view of the Cheltenham reservoir which looks like a flat blue lake. In summer it is edged with huge clumps of glowing rhododendrons, backed by conifers and seems as if it is part of a Gothic-style ballet.

Withington is a little village of surprising peace considering that it is so near the busy A40. A quiet country road passes a manor house on the left, with a sweeping drive and flowering shrubs on either side.

43

Colesborne. Look for the handsome stone house now turned into *Colesborne Inn*, covered with climbing roses and ivy. In the valley behind, the Churn ripples by. If you are, as the poem says, a 'lover of trees', you may enjoy Colesborne. There is a great house in the park where Henry Elwes lived; he was an authority on trees and planted many interesting and rare ones, including the Sequoia from American forests, and trees from the Himalayas. There is reputedly a larch growing by the river, which is such a rare place for a larch to flourish that when a German professor of botany, visiting Henry Elwes, saw it he exclaimed: 'There now, we must alter our text books.' But you *won't* see the rare trees without enquiring and spending a little time wandering in Colesborne. There are so many trees nearby that it is difficult to identify the unusual ones.

Cowley. When you leave the A435 you will find yourself cycling between stone posts, rather as if you were entering somebody's private park. You cycle along a fine avenue of beeches and presently round a slight incline to Cowley Manor. The Manor is set in formal grounds, with great yews and lawns, and the river Churn flows in the valley at the bottom of the hill. The Manor grounds are private, as the house is now an educational centre, but you *can* visit the tiny church, entering the churchyard through an arch cut in a high yew hedge. It's Alice in Wonderland's church, she used to visit the Rector here, he was a friend of hers.

As you cycle back down the hill, you'll probably see groups of young boys in boats on the little river. They are members of an Adventure Centre, and must have a lot of fun in this river-haunted country.

Cheltenham Tour Three

Total distance: 27 miles.
O.S. Map: 143.

Outward Route

Leave Cheltenham on the A4019 to **Uckington**. Turn right on to unclassified road to **Stoke Orchard**. Cycle to first right turn for **Tredington**. Cycle through Tredington to meet the A38, turning left into this road, then right on to B4213 to **Deerhurst**. In Deerhurst turn left to pass **Wightfields Manor** and **Apperley** where there is an inn by the river. Rejoin the B4213 at the next T junction, turn right to cross **Haw Bridge** to **Tirley**. Cycle straight through Tirley on B4213 for $\frac{3}{4}$ mile, then turn left on unclassified road (very winding) to **Hasfield**.

Homeward Route

Turn left in Hasfield for Tirley again, to recross the river by the Haw Bridge. After $\frac{3}{4}$ mile turn left off the B4213 on to unclassified road signposted for **Norton**. At T junction with A38, turn right and continue for one mile until you reach lefthand turn (unclassified road) for **Down Hatherley**. Continue on this road to join A40, turning left at T junction and cycling back on to main road into Cheltenham.

Stoke Orchard. It is rather built-up around here but the new houses are smart and rich-looking. In the distance you'll see Cleeve Hill, making a beautiful background to the little town. There are some timbered old houses and apple trees, and the place has a certain charm.

Tredington. We were determined to see the famous prehistoric fossil which surprisingly enough lies in the church porch. He is an ichthyosaurus and nine feet long. We found one needs quite a lot of imagination to turn this fossil into a recognisable creature – at first it looks like a rather interesting arrangement of variously shaped pebbles. But then you'll see the snout, pointing out of the porch, and later you'll be able to trace the body. Above it is a 'heel rubbing' done by someone interested a long time ago, and reduced down to a small photograph, which helps to identify the creature. Ichthyosaurs were fish lizards, rather like dolphins with large teeth. They came to the surface like porpoises, for air, had big eyes and probably keen vision. They lived 200 million years ago.

Deerhurst. This cycle trip is full of curiosities, and we came to Deerhurst on a typically British quest, to see the brass which shows 'the only *named* dog of fourteenth-century times'. His name, the history books told us, was Terri (with an 'i', not a 'y'). We found Deerhurst, Terri's village, at the end of a narrow lane. The church was hidden away among trees, and a young artist wandered among the gravestones drawing some of the elaborate decorations. There was a farm – and a tennis court – adjoining the church. The brasses are to the left in a chapel and set in the floor. There, sure enough, were Sir John and Lady Cassey and Terri. He's a very comic dog. He has a long face, wears a smile (as some dogs do!) and rolls up his eyes to look at his mistress with an expression of sentimental devotion. He's a sort of Walt Disney dog – you can imagine him talking. To match Terri, Sir John is accompanied by a worldly and pompous lion with a long curly mane like a girl's hair.

Outside the church, at the back, there are some excavations and a little sign which remarks: 'To the Angel'. High up on the ruined wall is the face of the only Saxon angel in England. The angel is strong and masculine and the carving, though faint, glares through the worn stone.

Deerhurst is a place of unique things. The dog. The angel. And two marvellous animal heads, on either side of the entrance porch. These are like figure-heads in Viking warships, wolves or boars yet with patterned faces and heads. When you touch the snout it is upward-curving.

Nearby, a step away from the church, is a notice which says 'Saxon Chapel: for key apply to black and white house adjoining'. The modest notice refers to Odda's Chapel, a miniature, near-perfect Saxon building curiously attached to a Tudor timbered house. Odda of Deerhurst was appointed Earl of Western Wessex in 1051, by Edward the Confessor's special favour. The chapel was built in 1056. Saxon treasures of this kind are rare.

Tirley. Look for the ancient clock on the tower of the church; its face is made of wood and the works are made up from bits and pieces of old farm tools – scythes, plough-shares and chain harrows.

Hasfield. By the church, behind fine stone walls, is the medieval home which once belonged to the Paunceforts. There's a romantic story about Dorothy Pauncefort who is supposed to have given up her right hand to ransom her imprisoned lover during the Civil War. Years ago her tomb was opened and the right hand actually was found to be missing. We looked across towards her old home which was peaceful but impressive.

Down Hatherley. Tiny church, lychgate, and many old houses here. You'll cycle through country like a park, flat and threaded by a broad river, with a notice warning swimmers away as the water is 'extremely dangerous'. Willows grow along the banks and many people fish here. A man with the curious name of 'Button Gwinnett' was born in this village. He was one of the people who signed the American Declaration of Independence in 1776 and his autograph was later sold for over £10,000.

This is a district of old red brick houses, apple trees, willows, and people walking by carrying fishing nets.

Detail from wall brass at Deerhurst

Cheltenham Tour Four

Total distance: 22 miles.
O.S. Map: 144.

Outward Route

Leave Cheltenham in the Andoversford direction for **Charlton Kings**. Turn left on to unclassified road for **Whittington**. Continue past the Roman Villa for **Syreford**. Turn left for **Sevenhampton**, cycling to **Brockhampton** and continue for one mile, taking first turn on right. Cycle for 1½ miles, then turn left again on to the **Salt Way**. Cycle along by the outer wall of Sudeley Park, descending by Sudeley Hill into **Winchcombe**.

Homeward Route

Cycling out of Winchcombe in the Broadway direction, take the unclassified road on right to **Sudeley Hill** and **Sudeley Castle**. Two miles' hard pushing will bring you to the top of **Round Hill**, then turn right and follow the **Outer Park Wall** and the **Salt Way** until you reach the turning on your right for **Brockhampton** and **Sevenhampton**. Rejoin Outward Route to **Syreford**, Whittington and Charlton Kings.

Charlton Kings. This village is already covered in Cheltenham Tour Two.

Whittington. The church is in an unusual place – it's on the lawn of the local manor house, Whittington Court, a stone Elizabethan house restored in Victorian times. There's a fourteenth-century font in the church, and sculptures of two knights and a lady. The knights are father and son, both with the local name of de Crupes. The knights are cross-legged, which – as they were Crusaders – means that, to quote an expert on the Crusaders whom we consulted, 'they did not die in their beds'!

Sevenhampton. This exceptionally peaceful and attractive village has many stone houses and cottages and is built on the banks of a small stream. If you like church brasses, look for John Camber in Sevenhampton's thirteenth-century church. He was a wool merchant and

48

a local benefactor, died in 1497, and wears a gown with those long sleeves, trimmed with fur, which you see in Shakespeare's plays about the Wars of the Roses. For a small fee one can obtain permission to do brass rubbings in old churches – it is a very fascinating way of taking home some stunning works of art many hundreds of years old. There is a Jacobean manor house just by the church.

Note for the energetic cyclist who enjoys archaeology.
This cycling trip is planned to lead you to Sudeley Castle which, to be thoroughly enjoyed, will take at least two hours. But if you are out cycling all day and enjoy both high places and Stone Age remains, cycle to Charlton Abbots (cars are not allowed in this quiet lane), and then climb the steep hill to Belas Knap. It is 1,000 feet up on the Cotswolds and there is a marvellous Long Barrow with burial chambers like caves dug out of the walls; in these walls the ancient chieftains were buried. The barrow has been restored and looks as it might have done over four thousand years ago.

Winchcombe. This lovely market town has many old houses and a galleried inn. On top of the restored church is a brightly gilded cock crowing triumphantly. And so he should, for this is where you'll see an extraordinary piece of Tudor history which still exists – a square of embroidery about $1\frac{1}{2}$ feet wide and framed under glass. It is a small portion of an altar-cloth actually embroidered by Queen Catherine of Aragon, Henry VIII's unhappy first queen. She had the reputation for being an exquisite needlewoman, and this altar cloth must have been very beautiful and elaborate. She embroidered it after her separation from the King. Her odd-shaped pomegranate badge, looking rather like a pineapple, is sewn in tarnished gold thread and thick applique along the borders of the embroidery.

Call at the *George Inn*. It was here in the Middle Ages that the pilgrims came, who were visiting St Kenelm's shrine. They stayed at the *George*, to sleep and refresh themselves, and you can still see the pilgrims' stone bath which is kept in the courtyard. The *George* has a gallery around the yard, and the beamed dining-room was where the pilgrims slept.

Sudeley Castle stands almost in the town, its grounds are reached down a short drive from the High Street. It is certainly one of the most fascinating houses we've visited in England, and it is small enough not to exhaust the visitor. We loved Sudeley Castle. There are ruins of the first castle built in the twelfth century, and other ruins of the Sudeley which was almost demolished during the Civil

War by the Roundheads. Yet much of the castle still stands, and it is fascinating. A small, elegant, comfortable home of a castle. In the gardens you'll see bright blue parrots who have real nests fixed for them, in barrels, in the trees. And there are wallabies, and peacocks, and lakes of water lilies.

The castle, in almost a thousand years, has more than once been a royal residence, and at least six kings and queens of England have stayed or lived here. In the fifteenth century Sudeley belonged to King Richard III, and later Henry VIII owned it and visited it with Anne Boleyn in 1532.

But the highest point of Sudeley's splendour came when the castle was given, by King Edward VI as a little boy, to his uncle Thomas Seymour. Seymour, who was a fascinating, sexually attractive and ambitious nobleman, married the widowed Queen Katharine Parr, within weeks of the King's death, and Sudeley then became her home. The castle was made ready, and Queen Katharine, with an enormous household (120 Gentlemen of the Household and Yeomen of the Guard), also brought Lady Jane Grey with her.

Poor ill-fated Jane lived there with Katharine, a happy, tranquil country life, until Queen Katharine died a year later bearing Seymour's little daughter.

The Queen is buried here in St Mary's Chapel. Her body lay here, from 1548 for 200 years, and it seemed that no one could remember where she was. But when the coffin was opened in 1782 the Queen's remains were found perfectly preserved – an ivy berry is said to have fallen into the coffin, sprouted and grown a crown of ivy round her head. The beautiful alabaster tomb where she lies now was designed by Sir Gilbert Scott in 1862.

We thought there were almost too many treasures to enjoy in the Castle, although it isn't large. But do look for the touching little white satin christening robe which was the infant Queen Elizabeth's. There are many varied relics, from tiny babies' bonnets of 200 years ago, embroidered gloves and kerchiefs. The paintings are magnificent – Holbeins, Turners, Rubens and many more. It is interesting that this wealth in treasures is due to the industry and love of a lady called Emma Dent. Her husband inherited Sudeley Castle from his uncles, three bachelors who had bought the castle in 1837; it was a gaunt, desolate ruin and a wreck covered in rubble and weeds. Emma devoted her whole life to continuing the work, started by the Dent brothers, of restoring Sudeley. She collected together its scattered treasures, documents and historical papers. She was its inspiration, and she's the reason that Royal Sudeley is Royal again.

Chipping Campden

It is typical, beautiful and, we're happy to say, totally unspoiled. There are numbers of fine old houses, including the late fourteenth-century Grevel's House and a delightful seventeenth-century Market Hall, now belonging to the National Trust. The remains of Campden House, burned in the Civil War, are impressive and still have a curiously sombre effect when you look at them. How the Civil War and its violence still lingers in this peaceful part of the world.

As in most Cotswold towns, there are some beautiful old alms-houses and one of the almost inevitable fifteenth-century 'wool' churches, as they're called. This one has a great 120-foot high tower, and inside you'll see a very interesting brass of William Grevel, presumably the owner of Grevel's House. He was called, somewhat ponderously, 'the flower of British wool merchants'. He certainly looks prosperous, in his merchant's clothes, and the brass has the fourteenth-century version of the 'wool mark' on it.

A mile north-west of Chipping Campden is Dover's Hill, a National Trust area, which is a marvellous viewpoint of the surrounding countryside. It is where the Cotswold Games used to be held – alas, they were discontinued long ago.

Before leaving visit the Bantam Tearooms for a salad or pâté lunch, or tea.

Tours from Chipping Campden

Chipping Campden Tour One

Total distance: 21 miles.
O.S. Map: 144.

Outward Route

Take the B4081 out of Chipping Campden in the Cheltenham direction. Fork right after half a mile on to unclassified road to Littleworth. Turn right at T junction and continue across next crossroads, climbing Dover's Hill to Weston Sub-edge. Leave in same direction, crossing the A46 and joining the B4035 for **Bretforton**. Fork right in the village for **South Littleton** (unclassified road). Just before South Littleton join the B4085 and continue cycling along this to **Cleeve Prior** and **Bidford-on-Avon**.

Homeward Route

Cycle back one mile on the same route to first cross-roads, turn left into unclassified road for **Barton**. Fork right after one mile for **Dorsington, Pebworth** and **Mickleton**. Visit **Kiftsgate Court** at Mickleton, then leave the village on A46 in Broadway direction, forking left almost at once on to B4081 home to Chipping Campden.

Weston Sub-edge. The village lies off the main road from Broadway to Stratford-on-Avon and is worth visiting. There are many ancient houses, some as early as the fifteenth century, and we saw a number with clipped yew hedges in the shape of birds. Latimer's House, one of the oldest in Weston, is where William Latimer and his friend Tyndale worked on translating the New Testament. The church has an interesting Elizabethan brass, a figure in the style of clothes that Shakespeare wore. And a magnificent cedar stretches over one of the oldest houses. There are certainly some fine manors round here.

South Littleton. Not all the places you pass through are interesting historically. Near South Littleton what impressed us was the market gardens. The road is flat and suburban with unremarkable bungalows, but the market gardens stretch along the left side of the road as you cycle towards Cleeve Prior, with orchards, fields of marrows, beans in flower in summer, onions, potatoes and asparagus. And beyond these, on the other side of Cleeve Hill, flows the Avon.

Cleeve Prior. The road is flat and an excellent one for spinning along quickly. There are wheatfields on either side and as you approach the village there's a new mixture of architecture, pink and white painted cottages and stone houses as well. The village is attractive and very quiet, with a pleasant inn, *The King's Arms*, which has an ancient dovecote at the back. The church is set in a little lane off the village green; we wanted to see the marks where the bowmen had sharpened their arrows on the church buttresses. These are at the foot of the tower on the left. They are extraordinary; you can put your fingers into the grooves worn by iron arrowheads – these marks seemed to us to be more *real* evidence of the past than many paintings or carvings. They were so haphazard and seemed strangely violent. The arrowheads were often as long as five inches and in late medieval times the shafts were a 'cloth yard' long.

The Manor is practically a village itself, with thick dark yews like a long tunnel from the gate, a thriving farm and a huge dovecote. We were told the manor has a hiding place from Civil War days – but alas, the house is not open to the public.

Bidford-on-Avon. The road is straight if a trifle hummocky and the views across the Vale of Evesham are fine, with orchards and fields of black-faced sheep. If you have time, look at Bidford's 500-year-old bridge over the Avon. Alongside you will find the *White Lion* pub and restaurant. Here you can have a snack in pleasant surroundings with a touch of tradition and modernity in the setting. There is a good view from the river here of boats and the church, and a pleasant little coffee shop called 'The Lion Cub', which belongs to the *White Lion*.

Pebworth. The village is full of black and white Tudor cottages, some thatched, and the whole village is beautifully kept – a kind of Elizabethan idyll. Of course the cottages in the past were lived in by villagers who farmed, were blacksmiths or woodcutters. Now many of these cottages belong to comfortably-off people who work in towns and return in the evening to their country retreats. Village life has completely changed. But for the cyclist looking for handsome and well-preserved villages, it's a pleasure to see cottages kept in this way. The Elizabethan manor behind its high walls is also beautiful.

CHIPPING CAMPDEN TOUR ONE

Broad Marston. It's almost next to Pebworth and there's a stone manor you'll admire as you cycle by, with three storeys of mullioned windows, lawns and an open drive. The tiny stream through the village is overgrown, and edged with thatched cottages.

Mickleton. There are Tudor houses here, and the church is set rather high on a hillock, approached by steps with a background of willows and elms. The little upper room of the porch has latticed windows; it's curious to think this was once a schoolroom for local children in the 1700s. The gardens of the manor house are close by the church, and everywhere in Mickleton in summer you'll see the long mauve and white spires of sweet-smelling buddleia.

Kiftsgate Court Gardens. This garden can be visited on Thursdays and Sundays from Easter to October, from 2 to 6. The view from the house drops down into a valley with many giant cedars. The garden, which has rare shrubs and plants, is enclosed in a series of retaining walls, and there are gates, pillars and climbing roses. It's specially famous for its collection of old and new roses.

Hidcote Manor Garden

Chipping Campden Tour Two

Total distance: 19 miles.
O.S. Map: 144.

Outward Route

Take the B4035 (Shipston direction), turn left after two miles and
follow signpost for **Hidcote Boyce** and **Hidcote Bartrim.** Visit Hidcote
House. Then fork right to **Lower Quinton**, riding through farmlands
with Meon Hill on your left. In Lower Quinton fork right for half a
mile, then take left-hand road up Harbour Hill to **Preston-on-Stour.**

Homeward Route

Take the Wimpstone and Newbold-on-Stour direction, with river
Stour on left; at Wimpstone turn right for **Ilmington**. At Ilmington
take the unclassified road towards **Darlingscott** and **Stretton-on-
Fosse**, turning right at the junction with the A4035, cycling home
through **Charingworth** and **Ebrington**, to Chipping Campden.

Hidcote House at Hidcote Bartrim. Your route passes a marvellous
Elizabethan house and you'll find the National Trust signs, with their
little green oak leaf insignia, easy to follow. The hedges in summer
are full of blue wild geraniums.

Hidcote Bartrim is a National Trust village and Hidcote Manor
gardens are superb. They are the most beautiful gardens we've seen
in the Cotswolds. It seems incredible that in 1905 there was no
garden here at all. Just one cedar, two groups of beeches, and some
fields. Hidcote Manor has noble stone gateways, a tiny family
chapel, and the Elizabethan house, rather tall and solid, is built on
three sides. There are dovecotes in the manor, the birdsong is loud,
and you'll see birds still flying in and out of nesting holes built in
Tudor times.

Now to the garden. It covers several acres, is really a succession of
gardens divided by clipped yew hedges, grassy walks and stone walls.
It is packed and crowded with flowers and shrubs, not an inch of soil
seems visible which is part of its originality. The hedges are marvellous, one harlequin hedge has five different trees growing in a kind

of pattern, box, yew, holly, beach and hornbeam. There are peacocks, doves and hens cut in clipped box, and little lily pools, stone busts and great hornbeam hedges which seem 'on stilts' because of the artful way they have been grown and trimmed. The gardens look secret which is part of their fascination; you go from one enclosed place of flowers and hedges to another, never quite sure what you will find blooming round the next garden corner. There's a fuschia garden, a stream garden, a pillar garden, a white garden and many others. In places Hidcote looks as beautiful as a painting by Watteau. And if you can manage to put them in your basket, you can buy plants here including the famous dark Hidcote blue lavender. Hidcote Manor gardens are open daily, Easter to October (except Tuesday and Friday) from 11 to 8. You can have tea in the restaurant here.

Ilmington. The road is straight between patchwork fields, the village lies by gently sloping pastures. This is a farming area with many orchards. The *Howard Arms* is a pleasant-looking stone inn and we also liked the look of the *Red Lion*. The village sprawls, with some new building, but the little road to the church is tiny and you may want to get off your bicycle and walk, passing two thatched cottages. The church, deep honey-coloured stone, is surrounded by fields crossed by footpaths. The huge yew in the churchyard has grown so large that it covers some of the graves, and there's a little vicarage in front of the church. Sage was in bloom when we visited Ilmington and the cottage gardens were full of roses and rosemary. We visited the church in search of any antiquity and found something very strange. It was a woman's figure in stone, life-size, her hands crossed, her eyes open. There is no card or notice to describe this figure which is so worn it could well be thirteenth or fourteenth century. But it has an eerie look propped against the wall of the belltower.

Ebrington. The village is on many different levels, the thatched houses have eyebrow doorways. Ebrington is full of flowers in summer, pansies, sweetpeas, balsam. The *Ebrington Arms* is small and stone-built, with bow windows. In the church we went to see the effigy of Lord Chancellor Fortescue, buried in 1476. He lies on a cushion, supported by two angels and a lion, and the effigy is painted in red and white, with a deep ermine collar and red painted roses. Fortescue's face is prim and strong, with a big straight nose and fourteenth-century hair in a smooth modern cut. He looks a tough, ironic man. There are marvellous views outside the church, stretching away into the distances.

Chipping Campden Tour Three

Total distance: 17 miles.
O.S. Map: 144.

Outward Route

Leave Chipping Campden on B4035 (Banbury direction), cycle through **Ebrington** and **Charingworth** until you come to first cross-roads after Charingworth. Turn left for Longdon Manor and fork left for **Ilmington**. Continue through Ilmington in the direction of **Stratford-upon-Avon**, and take first on the right for **Crimscote**. Fork right for **Talton House**. Turn left into A34, and right on to unclassified road up Ward's Hill to **Ettington**. Cycle to Stratford-upon-Avon on the A422.

Homeward Route

Leave Stratford-upon-Avon on the A34, cycling past Alscot deer park on your right to **Alderminster**. Continue on A34 to **Newbold-on-Stour**, forking right for **Armscote**. Continue cycling on unclassified road to **Darlingscott**, joining the A429 (Fosse Way) towards **Moreton-in-Marsh**. Turn right into the B4035 back through Charingworth and Ebrington to Chipping Campden.

Crimscote. The lanes curve gently and there are groups of trees on the horizon, but for a while there is not a building in sight. You cycle under elms, finally into the little village, passing fields full of grazing sheep. The village itself is very small, just some ancient barns, a few cottages and orchards.

Ettington. If you have time to call at *Ettington Park Hotel*, you will be visiting a house which was once the family manor of the Shirleys. This is built on the site of a seventeenth-century manor which was destroyed, but the church tower and one chapel has marvellous Shirley tombs and monuments, and there is some fifteenth-century glass in the windows which the Shirleys (who must have been a patrician lot) had moved from Winchester College when they decided to make the chapel the burial place for their family.

Stratford-upon-Avon. (This is covered in our Broadway Week-End Tour.) It seems rather presumptuous to list the treasures to be found in one of the most famous market towns in the world. But we've tried to add some details of places you may *not* have seen if you've already spent time in Stratford. Visitors usually start by walking under the limes to Holy Trinity Church. Some understanding person has put bicycle rests on the left of the churchyard path, so you will be able to leave your cycle there.

The church, which is extremely well cared for and rich-seeming, is visited all the year round by people who want to pay their respects to Shakespeare. His printed effigy looks down at you from the left of the chancel. Anthony Burgess, the well-known writer, described the bust as 'plump, complacent and faintly imbecilic.' This seems rather harsh, but we did agree that the man who sits there, holding a quill pen, doesn't look the genius he was. A photograph of the church register shows entries of his birth and death. He's described, with his date of burial, as 'Will Shakespere, gent'.

There is also in Holy Trinity a huge and magnificent tomb in the Clopton Chapel. George Clopton built the Clopton Bridge. It's maddening that one cannot get close enough to look at the figures and faces, although understandable that with the huge influx of visitors the chapel should be roped off. But four pairs of ghostly praying hands can be seen there, the men wear gold rings, and one of the ladies lying with her back to you is wearing the fashionable Paris veil.

When you've left the church, visit the Knot garden in Chapel Lane, a real Tudor garden with tiny box hedges in patterns, and flowers and herbs in brilliant sections, yellow and mauve, pink and flame-coloured. In the Guild Chapel, on the corner of Chapel Lane, you'll find one of the best Doom paintings in the district. It's extremely large and – what is so interesting – a Regency painter called Thomas Fisher did an impression of what the painting originally must have shown. As you gaze up at the naked chained souls being burned in hell, or the busy angels and the saved, you can actually match the design to the faded painting and make fresh sense out of it. The chapel was built originally in the thirteenth century by Robert de Stratford.

The Royal Shakespeare Theatre on the banks of the Avon is the world's most famous theatre; you may well know it and have visited it to see a Shakespeare play. But there is also their Picture Gallery close by, full of treasures including mementoes of Mrs Siddons, whose pearl-embroidered slippers can be seen, as well as Garrick's gloves, Irving's sword and scales used as Shylock, and many curious relics of theatre in the past. The paintings are fine and include a Fuseli, an Angelica Kaufman, and modern portraits of Laurence

Olivier, Paul Scofield, David Warner, Peggy Ashcroft and Edith Evans.

There are other marvellous things to see in Stratford, including the Birthplace, the old almshouse and Shakespeare's school, the Shakespeare Centre which is modern and has wonderful engraved glass panels, and the eighteenth-century Town Hall with an elegant statue to the poet. For visitors from the United States, Harvard House shouldn't be missed. It's a Tudor house in High Street, and the Harvard who built it had a son, John, who founded the famous American university.

Armscote. There's an old stone pub here with a pretty garden, many orchards with high old walls. Some of the cottages have lavender hedges. There is a distant view of low, blueish hills and we saw a gabled Tudor barn with a gatehouse over it, surrounded by fine ashes and poplars.

Darlingscott. This is a tiny place with a quiet air, the road gently sloping and big elm trees on either side. There are one or two small antique shops, and the old houses have stone roofs greyed with flowering lichen.

Chipping Campden Tour Four

Total distance: 26 miles.
O.S. Map: 144.

Outward Route

Leave Chipping Campden on the B4035 in easterly direction. Turn right into the A46 for **Mickleton.** Cycle through Mickleton, continuing on the A46 for threequarters of a mile, then fork left on to an unclassified road for **Broad Marston** and **Long Marston.** Then continue on the same road (due north) for **Welford-on-Avon.**

Homeward Route

Take the Barton direction from Welford, keeping the river Avon on your right, and take the second left turn for **Dorsington** and **Pebworth.** Join the A46 in Mickleton for quarter of a mile, then fork left on to B4081 for Chipping Campden.

Mickleton. It's a charming village with many Tudor houses and cottages, and if you have time visit the church, founded before William the Conqueror's time. There's a memorial in the church to the Graves family. John Richard Graves (whose father lived to be 103!) was a friend of Gainsborough, an amusing man, poet and essayist, much sought-after by the patrician families of the eighteenth century. Morgan, John's brother, was the squire at Mickleton Manor and if you look across the fields by the church you'll see an avenue of trees leading to Kiftsgate Court on the hill. It was planted by a poet friend of Morgan Graves.

Long Marston. The road is wide from Broad Marston to Long Marston, there are hills on the right and ahead of you. The trees look as if they could be in a Constable painting. As we came down the road, a line of geese flew overhead in a V formation. The village has whitewashed cottages and the church a beamed high bellcot.

There's a rose-coloured brick manor nearby. The old schoolhouse, of ivy-covered stone, is now a charming private house.

Welford-on-Avon. If you visit Welford in springtime, the Four Gables gardens are open to the public in April. The ornamental cherries and orchard should be full of blossom, with narcissus and daffodils, and there's a pleasant place for tea, *Apple Trees*, a pretty thatched cottage five minutes away.

The river is overgrown and full of rushes, and the winding road passes by good-style bungalows and rose gardens; the *Bell Inn* is very old, covered in virginia creeper and has a reputation for good food. Actors from Stratford's theatre sometimes visit the Bell.

Chipping Campden

Chipping Norton

The town first appears in history as the chief 'fief' of a Flemish baron who came over with William the Conqueror.

Chipping Norton is on the Cotswold ridge at the north rim of the Evenlode valley but has always been the most important centre of the valley. The word 'Chipping' means market which is what it was and still is. The town's Wednesday Market disappeared in the nineteenth century but it was revived again in 1958.

Chipping Norton, of course, was a wool town; a tweed mill still flourishes there and the attractive town retains its old personality. It has some excellent seventeenth-century almshouses, a lofty church with a clerestory which is almost all windows, and beautiful brasses.

The elegant Town Hall was designed, in 1842, by Repton with formal style, and nearby you'll see a number of eighteenth-century stone houses. The *White Hart* is a fine inn, worth visiting.

Altogether, with its attractive shops and a feel of past and present mingled, Chipping Norton is a pleasant place to stop.

Tours from Chipping Norton

Chipping Norton Tour One

Total distance: 22 miles.
O.S. Maps: 144, 145

Outward Route

Take the B4450 out of Chipping Norton for **Churchill**. Continue on this road until half a mile past **Kingham** Station. Turn left on to unclassified road for **Foscot, Bould** and **Idbury**. Turn left in Idbury on unclassified road for **Fifield**. Cycle through Fifield until left signpost to **Milton-under-Wychwood**. In Milton turn right for **Shipton-under-Wychwood**.

Homeward Route

Cycle back from Shipton to Milton, then take right fork for **Bruern Abbey**; leaving Abbey on your right, take the road in **Lyneham** direction for one mile. Turn left in Chipping Norton direction and rejoin the B4450 back into Chipping Norton.

Churchill. Warren Hastings was born in this little place; there's a handsome stone house where he was born. He is one of England's heroes who's always connected in our minds with a scandal – yet he was innocent. He saved India in the mid-eighteenth century when Governor of Bengal, strengthening justice, making the country safe from robbers and rebels. But he was unjustly impeached, as it was called, in Parliament on charges of corruption. There was a huge scandal which still reverberates through history books. The trial spread over seven years and cost Hastings over £70,000.

You'll see a monolith here to the memory of another famous man, William Smith, one of this country's notable geologists born in the village in 1767. He discovered the importance of fossils in fixing the ages of rock strata. There's also an arched fountain in the village.

Idbury. The village is on a hill and the views around are magnificent. We couldn't find the manor house which once belonged to Robertson Scott, the founder of The Countryman magazine, who loved the country and even let the swallows build their nests in his bathroom. We were told that over the front door of the manor are the words: 'O more than happy Countryman, if he but knew his good fortune'. It would be worthwhile looking for his house.

But we did find the tomb of Sir Benjamin Baker, the Victorian engineer who built the Forth Bridge, the Assuan dam in Egypt and worked on the first Undergrounds in London. He was an enormously successful late Victorian, a bit of a genius, and he's mentioned in the church as a local benefactor. It's curious to see his grave, an odd-shaped monument of four crossing arches, and to discover that none of his remarkable achievements are even mentioned. But there is his grave on this quiet hillside, facing a small church with a marvellous blocked-up doorway zigzagged with Norman patterns as fresh as if it had been carved yesterday.

Inside the church we found one single exquisite angel's face looking down from the top of a window of plain glass, a fragment left of a window perhaps 600 years old. And outside, on the front of the church, a rather irritable eighteenth-century angel in stone watched us leave.

Fifield. We wanted to see the village where Milton's youthful bride was born and grew up. Her name was Mary Powell and she was much too young and jolly at 17 to marry the stern, grave poet of Cromwellian times. Poor Mary pined for her Fifield home and 'much company and joviality' and left Milton after a month of marriage to go home. She didn't come back for two years. Fifield is still small and cosy, with a number of solid, homely Elizabethan and Stuart houses. The little church has a fourteenth-century steeple, and Mary must have worshippped there every Sunday.

You ride through **Milton-under-Wychwood** where a fair was being set up on the village green the day we visited it. It's a sprawling place, part old, part new, and you find yourself almost at once cycling into Shipton-under-Wychwood, for the villages run into one another.

Shipton-under-Wychwood. The *Shaven Crown Inn* is very interesting. It is big, handsome, with a Tudor gateway. It's built in stone with windows arched as if part of a church. The inn was originally built in the fourteenth century by the monks as a guest-house for the novices of Bruern Abbey, the earliest monastery to provide such comfortable accommodation for young student priests. We were told that the *Crown* has recently discovered yet another Tudor fireplace and that there's a secret passage – alas, it no longer works as a passage as the walls fell in.

There is a little enclosed courtyard filled with rose beds – a perfect place for a cycling stop. While you are in Shipton, visit the church to see a rare brass called a 'shroud brass'. It was sometimes the custom to make double-sided memorial brasses, on one side of which the figure is shown in a shroud. A memento mori. This brass quite small and framed in old wood, is in a corner of the church near the altar, attached to a pillar. On one side is Tudor writing, and the other shows Elizabeth Tame who died in 1548, lying in her shroud on a tiled floor. The shroud's in a sort of gathered knot on top of her long hair and by her feet. She's quite naked, her arching ribs showing clearly, yet the face looks perfectly serene, she actually looks alive lying in her shroud! What a pity the brass has become dark green with age; a notice says that no brass rubbings are allowed. Since many of the Cotswold brasses are available for rubbing at a small charge, and in consequence are a brilliant gleaming gold, it seems sad that Elizabeth must be left to her green covering of verdigris.

Bruern Abbey. You cycle across three bridges here where small boys enjoy fishing. The village is very small, built round a green and with a scattering of tiny cottages. The woods are full of elm trees, and tall poplars line the road. There is no sign of the medieval abbey which gave the place its name, nor could we find the fishpond which belonged to the monks. But the cycling is very restful and the country roads are level – the distant views are gentle and beautiful.

Chipping Norton Tour Two

Total distance: 20 miles.
O.S. Maps: 144, 145

Outward Route ·

Leave Chipping Norton on the A44 towards Moreton-in-Marsh. Cycle through **Salford** and one mile beyond the junction with the A436 turn left on to unclassified road for **Chastleton**. Turn right in Chastleton to return to A44 road for one mile, then turn left at **Four Shire Stone** on to unclassified road for **Evenlode**.

Homeward Route

Take road for **Adlestrop** until you meet the A436. Turn right. After ¾ mile turn left for **Oddington**. Cycle through Oddington in the **Maugersbury** direction until you meet the B4450. Turn left for **Bledington**. Cycle through Bledington for Kingham Station, returning to Chipping Norton by the B4450.

Chastleton House. This is covered, with other details about the house, in our weekend tour based from Northleach.

The house is on a hill, overlooking four counties, and was built only a year after the death of Queen Elizabeth. Yet it's essentially Jacobean rather than Tudor. Perhaps that's because of its connexions with the Cavaliers in the Civil War, for that unhappy time is still talked about at Chastleton, and still lingers on. It's as if, in some curious way, the sufferings, heroisms, plots and counter-plots, are somehow still there, still part of the formal rooms, still hanging in the embroidered bed-curtains.

Leave yourself enough time to go slowly round the house. It's very interesting and curious. It really does seem to have stayed unaltered since Charles I was on the throne. It was owned then by a family called Jones (it's still in the same family). They were passionately loyal to Charles and fought for him in the Civil War. In a room called the Cavalier's Room you can still see the secret chamber where one of the family was hidden when he'd ridden back, exhausted, after the Parliamentary troops sacked Worcester. There's

Chastleton House

a window in the secret room now – but it's still behind panelling.
The Roundheads saw the tired horse outside Chastleton House,
stormed in and searched but couldn't find the hidden Cavalier.
They waited all night, but his wife put opium in their ale, and when
they were senseless she helped her husband to escape. The house is
full of wonderful things – Charles I and his French Henrietta look
down at you from the formal dining-room, which is laid with Jacobean
glasses and plates, waiting for the king to arrive for dinner! There's
a bed-cover of elaborate white embroidery, Stuart patterned, that
took one of the girls *fifteen years* to finish. And the ceilings, as
elaborate, are patterned with pomegranates and leaves and flowers.

When you've been round the house, you can have tea in the
gardens, at the Brewhouse tearoom.

After visiting Chastleton you will rejoin the A44. Look out for
the big *Four Shire Stone* where you turn left for Evenlode. It's a
tall, golden stone with a ball on the top and stands back from the
road beside a hedge.

Evenlode. The road is straight but slightly undulating; you cross
the river Evenlode which is still only a small stream here. We saw
a sign for 'Pottery, visitors welcome'; it might be interesting to
buy pots from different parts of the Cotswolds – the local pottery
is attractive and very subtly coloured. Evenlode House, behind very

67

high walls, is Elizabethan, and can be seen through the gates. It faces the fourteenth-century church. There are two rarities to enjoy in this little church. One is a 'Sanctus' chair, a great heavy stone chair rather like the Coronation chair in Westminster Abbey. 'Sanctuary people' as they were called, were those escaping from persecution or trouble. Once inside a church, no one could touch them. This Christian law began in England in 399 and wasn't repealed until 1723. Apparently when you claimed sanctuary you sat in the Sanctus chair. The chair was made either in 1200 or 1300, and one of its arms has a great ball on the end, carved with a deep cross and polished by how many hundreds of hands of people in danger. There are only three chairs like this in England.

High in one of the tiny windows is a portrait of Edward the Confessor. He has a strong face, with a curled beard and a blue velvet hat which is surrounded by his halo. He seemed to us a kind of British apostle.

Adlestrop. The village has a haunting name; to thousands of people it only means a poem by Edward Thomas, one of the Great War poets killed in the trenches. One hot summer afternoon before that long-ago war, his train stopped unexpectedly at a little lost country station; the poem begins

> 'Yes, I remember Adlestrop –
> The name, because one afternoon
> Of heat, the express train drew up there
> Unwontedly . . .'

In those days Adlestrop must have been a very lost village indeed, quiet as in a spell. The railway line still passes nearby but the spell has gone. There are a lot of new houses being built in Adlestrop. We looked through the gates of Adlestrop House, just by the church. It's in Cotswold stone and Elizabethan, but we couldn't see the famous gardens designed by Repton, the landscape gardener who helped to design Kensington Gardens. All we saw were spreading cedars. But we did find the stone house, once the Rectory, where Jane Austen used to visit her friends.

Bledington. The village, which is also on the Evenlode river, has a spacious village green and a Victorian maypole! There it stands, topped by a running fox which is also a weathervane. There are beautiful views of Maugersbury Hill as you cycle along these quiet roads.

Chipping Norton Tour Three

Total distance: 22 miles.
O.S. Map: 145.

Outward Route

Leave Chipping Norton by the A361 in the Witney direction. Fork left on to unclassified road for **Chadlington**. Continue on this unclassified road, crossing the B4437 and cycling through the Wychwood Forest to **Leafield**. Turn left into unclassified road for Finstock, running along the edge of the forest.

Homeward Route

Turning left after visiting **Finstock**, in half a mile you will join the B4022 and after cycling another half a mile you cross the Evenlode river near Fawler. Continue on B4022 to **Charlbury**. After visiting **Charlbury**, rejoin the B4022 back to Chipping Norton through **Spelsbury** and the quiet countryside.

Chadlington. The village is near what is left of Wychwood Forest and there's a stately manor behind yews and surrounded by huge trees. You'll see its tall chimneys as you cycle by. The church, beside the road, has amusing gargoyles as well as heads of knights, princes of the church, little grimacing peasants, priests and dragons. There is nothing else remarkable about the church (except a little doorway built in the 1200s) but the views are breathtaking along this road. Near Chadlington is a trace of a Viking camp. In Saxon times the Danes often invaded this part of the country in search of slaves and booty, and you can see the earthworks of one of their camps here.

Leafield. It's at the top of the valley between two rivers, the Windrush and the Evenlode, a small village not far from Wychwood Forest, now a National Nature reserve. Wychwood was once a huge forest which covered the countryside and stretched from Woodstock to the Windrush valley. It was a royal game forest; as far back as King Canute nobody could hunt here but the king. This wasn't just because royalty enjoyed sport – they badly needed venison and other game to be had in the forests to feed the huge gatherings of knights and retainers who accompanied the king wherever he travelled. Wychwood has now shrunk to small but beautiful woods, rich in flowers and small creatures. A stoat ran across our path, and in the dusk sometimes a few rabbits scuttled into the hedges.

Spelsbury. It's a charming quiet Oxfordshire village, with winding roads and woods which stretch away into the distance. The village is on a rise among elms. The church is on a 'No through road', close to a fine Jacobean vicarage, and from the churchyard there are distant views of fields, hedges and low hills.

We liked the church very much; it's light and cheerful and well cared for, with a pleasant smell of furniture polish! There's a marvellous monument to the Lee family, under a white canopy and six pillars. They are dressed in elaborate Stuart clothes with heavy lace collars (the style worn by Charles I), ribbons, laces, bows and full sleeves. Sir Henry Lee wears armour, his wife a veil and an elaborate dress, and round them are seven little children, four nearly grown up, one son in armour with his hand on his heart, and three little babies, one in a cot. We've often thought the babies in these carved memorials very sad – they must be the images of children who died in infancy. Yet the artists of sepulchres in the past *before* Victoria's reign never seemed to give death a gloomy aspect. The children kneeling round their parents in the Lee memorial, and even the babies arranged in a tidy row in front of them, could not possibly depress you. They seem like a sculpture of a living family.

Look round for Viscount Dillon, he's in the north chapel, a figure in a robe trimmed with fur. We also discovered a piece of beautiful tapestry hanging on the church wall. There was no notice to explain it but it looked very old, possibly Elizabethan. It showed the figures of two young girls in a garden, one standing and one sitting. One girl has a bird on her finger and they're in a field full of flowers, birds, squirrels, magpies, rabbits and – most interesting – a lion and a unicorn on either side of them. We wondered if the tapestry represented the young Elizabeth and her sister Mary Tudor when they were teenage princesses.

Taston. If you cycle a little off your route from Spelsbury, taking the unclassified road on the right, you'll find the small village of Taston. We were looking for the famed Thor Stone and found it, to our surprise, apparently leaning casually against a garden hedge. It's over six feet high, jagged and pitted, but untouched by any sign of being made by man. It is called the Thor Stone after the northern god of thunder – and that's all anyone could tell us about it. Somehow its prehistoric magic seemed lost – it looked very domesticated by that garden.

Chipping Norton Tour Four

Total distance: 26 miles.
O.S. Map: 145.

Outward Route

Leave Chipping Norton on B4026 for **Over Norton,** turning left in village on to unclassified road, crossing the old railway line. Turn sharp right at the next crossroads for the **Rollright Stones.** Continue cycling in same direction, crossing the A34 until you come to a right-hand turn for **Great Rollright.** Leave the village by the Hook Norton road (easterly) then turn sharp left into the village of **Hook Norton.** Turn right and then left, continuing on unclassified roads in northerly direction for **Sibford Ferris** and **Sibford Gower.**

Homeward Route

Turn right in Sibford Gower and right again on to B4035; after a very short distance turn right on unclassified road to **Wigginton** and **South Newington.** Leave by the A361 in Chipping Norton direction, and after two miles fork left on to B4022 for **Great Tew.** Following unclassified road out of Great Tew, through **Little Tew,** back to A361 to return to Chipping Norton.

The Rollright Stones. This extraordinary prehistoric stone circle with no ditch round it is one of England's mysteries. It belongs to a past from so long ago that there are few traces of the men who made it. Experts say the circle was made about 1,500 years before Christ and must have a ritual meaning. The men who made these stones (which were definitely cut from local limestone) were of the Bronze Age. They made their camps and trade routes across high places for safety, clear of the forest which covered most of the country. The circle looks like a ring of witches turned into stone; the stones, deeply pitted and pocked by the weather, are of varying heights, which must have been deliberate, some the size of a man, others tiny stumps. The circle is second in importance, archaeologically, to Stonehenge and Avebury; it retains great power and strangeness.

On the other side of the road is the King's Stone, which someone said looks like a rearing cobra. It does. It stands alone, its top – the snake's hood and head, so to speak – broader and heavier than the base. In another field on the right, not far from the circle, are a group

71

with the name of 'The Whispering Knights'. An old English legend says they were knights who plotted against the king leading his army and all were turned to stone by a witch. We thought the medieval names for these savage relics very unsuitable. A wind blows strongly here on top of the ridge – you're on the roof of Oxfordshire in a place where once bears, wolves and boars roamed.

Hook Norton. As you cycle through the village, it is worth stopping to visit the church which has a rather oddly carved font, of Norman times, heavy and tub-shaped, with the figures of Adam and Eve in gardening mood with spade and rake; Eve holds the apple and they are standing by the tree of life. The church has pinnacles and a flag flies. It is surrounded by gardens and has an old gilded sundial on the roof under the eaves. There are pretty thatched cottages in the village and weeping willows by a stream.

Sibford Gower. The country is hilly and wooded and the deserted road haunted with birds. We saw a lot of goldfinches flying from hedge to hedge and passed a farm with a yew quite 30 feet high, a huge solid mass of dark green. The *Wykeham Arms* pub looks comfortable with a promising sign saying 'Good Food and Hospitality'.

South Newington. You may be interested to see a collection of fourteenth-century wall paintings in the church; these were done by a group of travelling artists who went from village to village, painting church walls. One of the paintings is of Thomas à Beckett's murder, the knights attacking, a priest protecting him. Once again a sign that Beckett's murder wasn't forgotten – how often it's repeated in Cotswold church art.

To encourage the wool trade, so vital to the area, a law was passed in the Middle Ages which made it obligatory for bodies to be buried in wool. On the wall of this church you'll see framed oaths taken which witnessed that the law had been kept.

Great Tew. It's the kind of village you see on sentimental calendars. An enchanting place, with thatched cottages, a village green, everything cosy and close. We had been fascinated by the story of Lucius Carey, Viscount Falkland, who lived here at Great Tew during the Civil War, and we came in search of a memorial to him.

Falkland often stirs people's imagination. C. V. Wedgwood, the historian, calls him 'gentle Lord Falkland, this intelligent and upright man'. One of his friends described him as 'of a wit so sharp and a nature so sincere that nothing could be more lovely'.

He was the epitome of the gallant cavalier who fought for his king; courageous, rash, a poet, a beloved friend. But he detested the Civil War and was deeply depressed by it for he had friends on both sides. In the end, still fighting loyally for Charles I, he practically committed suicide by deliberately riding against the Roundhead guns, at a critical moment in the Battle of Newbury. In *Brief Lives*, John Aubrey, a contemporary of Falkland's, wrote that he did not believe the gallant myth, adding: 'I have been well enformed . . . by those that best knew him, and knew the intrigues behind the curtaine (as they say) that it was the death of Mris. Moray, a handsome lady at court, who was his mistress, and whom he loved above all creatures, was the true cause of his being so madly guilty of his own death'. Two stories. Which is true?

After the battle his body was brought secretly to the manor here at Great Tew and buried, otherwise Cromwell's soldiers would have stolen and decapitated it. The vicar told us no one knows where his mother buried her son but, said the vicar simply, 'we still remember his soul'.

We went, inevitably, to the church. You must cycle up a hill from the village, passing Falkland Manor on the left. The house has been rebuilt since Lucius lived there, but the gardens are his own. To get to the church you go through an elaborately carved stone gateway, exactly like an entrance to the manor park. The path is edged with lawns and trees, and in the summer you'll smell limes in flower. In the church we found some young Americans busy taking brass rubbings from three sets of fifteenth-century brasses (they're very good ones and shouldn't be missed). But all there is in the church to commemorate the Cavalier is a modern wall monument put up not long ago. The vicar told us that 'some of Lucius's friends collected some money between them'.

But there *is* a contemporary monument to Lucius. It's in Burford church, curiously enough. He's wearing green and gold armour and kneels near his mother. A very odd bust of his wife is beside him. The face in his monument isn't at all the way one imagines Lucius Falkland. His face, with neat moustache, looks much too young – twenty, perhaps. And it's blank and rather weak like that of an old-time film star. He must have been much more of a man than that, handsomer, more alluring. But go and look at him if you're in Burford for he is one of the Cotswolds' heroes.

Little Tew. You will cycle through a countryside of small dips and hollows and little hills, and the village itself is tiny and quiet, with stone cottages and farms.

Cirencester

Somehow everybody seems to know that Cirencester was a Roman town, and not only because of its name-ending. It grew up, understandably, because during the Roman occupation it was in a place of considerable strategic importance. It was at the junction of three great Roman roads – the Fosse Way, Akeman Street, and the westerly of the two Ermine Streets. You'll still cycle on all three of these arrow-straight roads today. Cirencester became, almost certainly, the second city of Britannia; it was the capital of one of the four provinces into which the Emperor Diocletian divided Britain at the end of the 3rd century.

You'll see many marvellous Roman relics in the Corinium Museum* in Park Street. All the Roman antiquities at the Museum have been found locally, including mosaic pavements and – even more interesting – Roman sculptures of people who once lived in Cirencester. It's open on weekdays, July to September, mornings and afternoons until 5.30, and from October to June until 4.30. Sunday during the summer only. In Cotswold Avenue is another very curious thing – a stepped depression once part of the town's amphitheatre.

Although it never became as important again as when the Romans lived here, Cirencester didn't disappear from history. There's a St John's Hospital built by Henry I, and it had an abbey, which Henry VIII dissolved ... a gateway is all that is left. Cirencester has a magnificent church with a three-storeyed porch carved as elaborately as lace, and a pinnacled, graceful tower, 135 feet high.

Cirencester was a wool town and has a number of beautiful old inns and the old Weaver's Hall. Four miles south-west of the town is Thames Head Bridge, just by the Tewkesbury Road. It is usually accepted (of course, people dispute this) to be the source of the Thames. It's marked, as you would expect, by a statue showing Old Father Thames.

*The Corinium Museum has recently been doubled in size, There is also a site of a Roman town house in Cirencester where you can see the way the Romans laid their ornate mosaic floors.

Tours from Cirencester

Cirencester Tour One

Total distance: 18 miles.
O.S. Map: 157.

Outward Route

Leave Cirencester by the A419 in the direction of **Cricklade**. Take a right turn (unclassified) for **Siddington**. Cycle down this road for three miles to **South Cerney**. Turn left in South Cerney on an unclassified road which follows round the side of water. Continue on this road to **Cerney Wick**. Turn left out of Cerney Wick, crossing the river Churn, and after one mile cross the A419 road and head for **Down Ampney**. Outside Down Ampney fork right for **Meysey Hampton**.

Homeward Route

Leave Meysey Hampton in a northerly direction, crossing the A417 and cycling to the hamlet of **Sunhill**. Turn left and cycle for one mile to **Betty's Grave**. Cross an unclassified road and head for **Ampney St Mary**, forking right at next junction. On leaving Ampney St Mary bear west for **Ampney Crucis**, then riding through the village, bearing south in the direction of Ampney park and turning right on to the A417 back into Cirencester.

Siddington. On your way to this village you are cycling through a countryside bordered by 'stone hedges'. And white doves stand cooing on grey stone roofs. Alongside the church is a cottage nestling in its vegetable and flower garden. When we saw it, the path to the front door was bordered by great clumps of purple and yellow violas. Behind a row of lime trees were the high Elizabethan chimneys of a beautiful manor.

But the most intriguing things we found here were on the porch of the church. Those stone beak-heads again! The Siddington ones are the best we saw in the Cotswolds, because the sculptor thought they were so funny. Some of these beak-heads actually had little mischievous hands stretched out to grip the noses or beaks of their neighbours. One was giving a distinct pull to his neighbour's curved beak. Another looked like a wicked owl. Don't miss these.

South Cerney. On the route to this village, a good smooth road for cycling, is a little isolated stone tower on the right of the road outlined against the horizon, like a miniature fort in Scott's Ivanhoe. In the village is a riverside walk on the banks of the Churn, (a tributary of the Thames) with the odd name of 'Bow Wow' – perhaps a favourite walk for the dogs of the village? The river in summer is covered with white flowers, and an attractive pub, *The Eliot Arms*, faces the water.

Meysey Hampton. Elms line the road and there are magpies and goldfinches flying around. A good stop is the *Mason's Arms*, a golden stone house over 200 years old with a welcoming host. Have a snack in the Creamery, which has real country atmosphere and is comfortable and inexpensive.

If you enjoy curious monuments and their history, call at the thirteenth-century church and have a look at Doctor James Vaulx. He was physician to James I (Mary Queen of Scots' son), and his monument shows him with *both* his wives and sixteen little children. The monument is 15 feet high, and an inscription says 'None but Vaulx can lye below'.

Betty's Grave. There it is on the map, this quiet crossroads with its curious name. It is overshadowed by beeches and is a windy, lonely place. It's supposed to be the grave of Elizabeth Bastoe who died in 1786; all the stories about her differ. One says she was a witch and was hanged or burned. Or she was hanged for stealing sheep, or she died of exhaustion after challenging a man that she could hoe a field faster than he could. We could find no trace of Betty's grave today but the name endures.

Ampney St Mary. It is a place of walled gardens, with a delightful sign 'Danger, children, horses and dogs crossing'. Oddly, the church is a mile out of the village. It's said this is because the Black Death swept through Ampney and the villagers moved away to avoid the plague. The church was left isolated in green fields. You'll find it just off the A417 and you have to walk along a grassy footpath. It's locally called 'The Ivy Church' because before it was restored in 1913 it was covered all over with ivy. There's a fourteenth-century elm door, and a bell with the beautiful inscription 'Peace and Good Neighbourhood'. It's a very simple, almost severe church, yet faint frescoes hint at bright colours long ago. One little face, painted in the thirteenth century, looks down at you from the arch of a window. The day we called, the church was full of flowers, both cottage flowers and wild ones. And outside, over a blocked doorway, we saw a marvellously clear-cut sculpture of a lion and a serpent fighting.

Ampney Crucis. The village is one of those long straggling groups of cottages with flowery gardens – grey stone walls covered in pink valerian. Look for *The Old Bakery* which serves coffee and delicious Cream Teas.

In the turreted church is the statue of George Lloyd wearing a Tudor ruff, and his wife who wears that distinctive and fashionable headdress of the time called a 'Paris veil'. Many of the ladies with monuments in the Cotswolds wear this headdress which was certainly very becoming. Below the Lloyds are 13 prim little figures, surely their children.

Cirencester Church Tower

Arlington Row, Bibury

Old Vicarage, Quenington

Cirencester Tour Two

Total distance: 19 miles.
O.S. Map: 157.

Outward Route

Leave Cirencester by the A433 in the direction of **Bibury**. Cycle three miles along the main road then turn right along the unclassified Roman Road, **Akeman Street**, for **Quenington**. At Quenington turn left for **Coln St Aldwyns**. Turn left again for **Bibury**.

Homeward Route

Leave Bibury by the unclassified road to **Ablington** (northerly direction). Turning left, the road crosses the river Coln and takes you to **Winson** and **Coln Rogers**. Turn left and head south for **Barnsley** which you reach after cycling three miles (cycling along the edge of Barnsley Park on your left). Turn right into the A433 and cycle back to Cirencester.

Quenington. This is a breathtakingly beautiful corner of England, with every house in the grey stone Cotswold tradition. At the entrance of Quenington Court is a circular dovecote, with fluttering and cooing birds flying in and out. Close by stands a tall, impressive stone gatehouse of Norman times. This was once part of the dwellings of the Knights Hospitallers; it's odd to record that these people were military monks. To present-day ideas, the juxtaposition of a priest and a soldier seems an odd one. But the Knights Hospitallers was founded in Jerusalem in the eleventh century to care for poor pilgrims, and then became connected with the Crusaders and a bulwark of Christianity in the East.

Further along the lane in Quenington, passing beautiful ancient houses, you'll come to the church.

St Swithin's Church stands back from the quiet lane in a churchyard full of yellow potentillas. The Norman doorway is surrounded with carvings of zigzags and daisies, and there's a fine sculpture of Christ with three kneeling figures whom we thought must be apostles.

The road from Quenington to **Coln St Aldwyns** is a rolling road, up and down, passing through green wooded country, full of beeches. Horses look at you as you cycle by. We noticed a pleasant pub, the *New Inn*, by the river, with willows growing beside it.

Bibury. The *Swan Hotel*, once a seventeenth-century coaching inn, faces the rushing river Coln which runs fast over stones and down a small waterfall of little steps. The river here is diverted to make a stream encircling the hotel garden. You can eat fresh-caught trout at the *Swan* if you feel a little extravagant; the fish comes from the trout farm opposite. Or, if you are more soft-hearted, why not feed the trout? They swim in a series of man-made pools by the bridge, with ducks and moorhens. And you can buy fish food for 5p a bag. Or, if you visit the impressive seventeenth-century Arlington Mill behind the trout-farm pools, you can see the fish swimming in the millrace which is illuminated with lights under the water. Arlington Mill once made tweed and flour, and still has all its machinery in working order. It is now a country museum with William Morris-style costumes, Staffordshire china and agricultural implements. William Morris loved Bibury, and wrote to his sister to say that it was 'the most beautiful village in England'.

Don't forget to look at the lovely Arlington Row of cottages, regarded as perfect examples of Cotswold village architecture, and situated on rising ground with woods behind them. Some Americans once wanted to buy these and ship them back to the States, stone by stone. Happily, this idea was turned down!

Winson. Check before you go on this cycling tour to find out whether Winson Mill Farm gardens are open. You may be able to visit these riverside gardens, which are in a particularly beautiful setting on the Coln.

Coln Rogers. The church is Saxon and is said to be one of the best of its kind in Gloucestershire. If you are interested in very ancient stained glass, look for St Margaret, who wears a crown and stands on a dragon. There's a very small Saxon window in the chancel which has been carved out of one large stone.

Barnsley. There's a perfect house here, someone's home and not a museum, whose gardens you can visit during the summer on certain days. Worth checking. The garden has shrubs, herbacious borders, a pond garden, a laburnum walk and an eighteenth-century summerhouse. It is the Old Rectory (now Barnsley House) and dates from the seventeenth-century. You can also visit The Dower House for its gentians, or The Furlongs for its roses and peonies.

Barnsley is a winding place of stone houses, gardens and rock gardens.

Cirencester Tour Three

Total distance: 25 miles.
O.S. Maps: 157, 144.

Outward Route

Leave Cirencester by the A417 in the Gloucester direction through
the **Spital Gate**, turning right outside the gate on to the White Way
(unclassified road). Cycle about five miles through lovely countryside bordering the North Cerney Downs, then turn left to **North
Cerney**. Turn right on to the A435 for $1\frac{1}{2}$ miles, following the winding route of the river Churn, then turn right on to unclassified road
for **Rendcomb**. Cycle back to the A435 and return to North Cerney,
then take left turn, forking right after quarter mile for **Calmsden**.
Turn left for **Chedworth**. Follow the signpost to the right for **Yanworth**, skirting round the edge of Chedworth Woods to the site of
the Roman Villa, which is very well signposted.

Homeward Route

Cycle round the edge of Chedworth Woods along valley of river Coln
in north-westerly direction, turning left and cycling through woods,
past disused airfield, and back to Chedworth Laines. Return on the
White Way which you have now rejoined, to Cirencester.

North Cerney. The 800 year old church is rightly famous. It is small
and stands on a little rise in a well-kept churchyard. What a church
of odd faces it is! Solemn ones look down at you from the tops of
windows, gargoyles grimace, and inside the church is a fat monk, a
serious queen, and a jolly king with luxuriant moustaches. There
is also a beautifully painted balcony. But)perhaps the strangest
faces belong to the figures carved, but growing each year fainter,
on the outside walls of the church. These have the quality of cave
drawings, they are bold and almost obscene. This is real pagan art,
showing men who are half animals, centaur-men with horns, looking
at you with sexy, knowing grins. One wonders how the powerful and
solemn Church of the early centuries allowed these carvings.

We liked the look of the *Bathurst Arms*, facing the church across
the main road. Its grassy lawns lead down to a little stream, and it has
an air of comfort.

At Chedworth

North Cerne

Rendcomb. This village is high on a headland, with deep valleys on either side of it. If you are interested in stained glass, do visit the early sixteenth-century church. The glass is Flemish and well worth seeing.

Chedworth Roman Villa. It's called Chedworth but the villa is nearer to Yanworth. The road there is one for nature lovers; we saw rolling country, cattle and sheep grazing together, magpies, swallows and pheasants. Chedworth has streams running through old meadows, thick woods, fields of wheat and parkland with huge oaks.

The Villa, which is the property of the National Trust, was first discovered a hundred years ago by a gamekeeper digging for rabbits. No Roman villa in the west of England is as completely excavated as Chedworth. The villa dates from the middle of the second century when the Romans had already been in Britain for 150 years. Owners of villas like this one were Romanised Britains who lived as country gentlemen. Their houses were elaborately decorated, well built and very comfortable. The rooms were heated and had Roman baths. At Chedworth you'll see superb mosaic floors. We were captivated by those of the dining-room, which used the favourite Roman motif of the four seasons. Winter's figure has a woollen pixie hood, heavy socks, and he carries a branch of dead leaves, and a hare for the stockpot.

The complicated suite of dressing-rooms and hot and cold bath-rooms, some like present-day Saunas, some like Turkish baths, take up a surprising amount of the villa space. What luxury! The sequence of how you took these baths in Roman days particularly fascinated some American visitors while we were there. They stood for a long time working out how the heat was graded from warm to very hot, and the bather then, bathed in perspiration, moved into the rooms which slowly cooled his skin, finally plunging into a cold bath to close the pores.

Chedworth is a place you can't visit in a hurry. When you cycle there, give yourself plenty of time to study the spacious rooms and the plan of the whole building, and to visit the museum. In that quiet spot you will actually be able to imagine the Roman life in the Cots-wolds in a time that seems so remote as almost never to have happened.

Cirencester Tour Four

Total distance: 24 miles.
O.S. Maps: 144, 157.

Outward Route

Leave Cirencester on the A417 in the direction of Gloucester, turning left half a mile after **Stratton** on the unclassified road for **Daglingworth**. Cycle on the same road, past **Duntisbourne Rouse**, **Duntisbourne Leer**, to **Duntisbourne Abbots**. Turn left, and after one mile turn right for **Winstone**, still on an unclassified road. Go right into the village of Winstone itself, then, after visiting it, return on to your previous road for **Caudle Green** and **Brimpsfield**.

Homeward Route

Turn left in Brimpsfield, cycling towards **Cranham**, but after two miles turn left on to the B4070 and follow this road for ¾ mile before forking left on to unclassified road called Calf Way.

Continue on this road for Bisley. Fork left in Bisley for Water Lane and **Sapperton**, crossing the river Frome just before Sapperton and climbing up through the woods. Continue on this road until you meet the A419. Turn left and follow this main road back into Cirencester.

Daglingworth is a calm and friendly place, with a fine square Georgian house right next door to the church. The day we called, there were some Cotswold craftsmen repairing the church roof and smiling down at us from a high ladder. The church looks over cornfields, and there are rolling hills in the distance.

We liked the brass tablet which is in the porch. It is to 'Giles Handcox' who left his soul to Heaven, his love to his friends and, to the poor, five pounds 'for their best advantage and releefe'. It's interesting that the next generation of Handcoxes had altered their spelling to Hancock, the modern version.

The tower of the church, which is fifteenth century, was partly built by nuns, who must have been rather brave and not given to vertigo. We looked all around for the famous stone from a Roman altar. It's said to be outside the vestry and carved in Latin, dedicated by Junia 'to the Mother and Genius of this place'. It's a poetic idea but there was no trace of the lady that we could see.

Duntisbourne Abbots, Rouse and Leer. All three of these villages have houses with lovely gardens which are open to the public at certain times in the summer. Check these before you set out on your trip.

Brimpsfield. Monks lived once in this village, there are the foundations of a priory near the church. And in the eleventh century the family of the Giffords, known as the 'fighting Giffords' had a great castle here. But King Edward II destroyed the castle and hanged John Gifford, one of the barons fighting against him. Nothing is left of this bloody history but a grassy mound and foundations of a few walls and gateway. Brimpsfield is now a small stone-built village, beginning to grow with a number of new stone houses.

Bisley. If you're here on Ascension Day you may be lucky enough to see the well dressing ceremony. Three gardens here are open to the public in the spring and early summer. Over Court, which was granted to Queen Elizabeth as part of her estate, has what is described rather charmingly as a 'tapestry hedge' – it means different colours and different varieties to give a patterned effect. And at the William and Mary House of Jaynes Court there's an eighteenth-century cockpit. Near Bisley is Lypiatt Park where the Gunpowder Plot conspirators met.

Sapperton. John Masefield, the poet, lived here for many years in a farmhouse called Pinbury Park. His house overlooks a lovely wooded valley. A poem that Masefield wrote about Dick Whittington must have been written when he lived here; it has the authentic feel of the countryside:

> 'He trudged the lambless Cotswolds, wintry-drear,
> Saw Lechlade's shadows in the floods of Thames,
> Dared the wind-haunted downlands with no names.'

Pinbury Manor in the time of Cromwell's son was the home of Sir Robert Atkyns. He was one of those upright men in a society given to some corruption in high places, who proved to be an embarrassment to his friends and, at the King's Restoration, to the Court. He was shocked by pensions for Members of Parliament and opposed them, and refused money sent him by the King. Finally he was pushed out of his post as Recorder of Bristol, and spent his life at Sapperton.

85

Cricklade

It is on the boundary between the Cotswolds and the Vale of White Horse, and has wonderful antiquities to enjoy, although the town is not important historically. It was, in Saxon times, a fortress rather similar to the fortress of Wallingford, a rectangular enclosure surrounded by a bank and a ditch, to protect its crucial ford.

There is a lovely church, St Sampson's, with a tower built in the sixteenth century and one of those elaborately vaulted roofs; nearby is the old gabled school. Oddly enough, the people in Cricklade tell you that the most unusual thing in their town is Queen Victoria's clock tower. It was erected to celebrate her Diamond Jubilee, and the pendulum swings in water.

Tours from Cricklade

Cricklade Tour One

Total distance: 20 miles.
O.S. Map: 157.

Outward Route

Leave Cricklade by the A419 in the Cirencester direction, turning
right after ¾ mile on to the unclassified road for **Marston Meysey**.
Returning from Marston Meysey to the same road which you have
followed from Cricklade, cycle left for ¾ mile, then right to **Castle
Eaton** and **Hannington**, continuing in a southerly direction until you
meet the B4019. Turn left and cycle into **Highworth**.

Homeward Route

Come out of Highworth on B4019 in Blunsdon direction. After
3½ miles your road crosses the A419. Turn right, and immediately
left, on to unclassified road for **Blunsdon St Andrew**. Cycle through
Blunsdon St Andrew on the same road until you meet the B404,
turn left for **Widham** and **Purton**. Return to Cricklade by the B404.

Marston Meysey lies on a quiet little road, one of the unclassified
roads which surround Fairford Airfield, the test place of Concorde.
It's a pleasant, quiet village of trim cottages with a well-kept air.
Down a side turning is a pub called the *Spotted Cow* which offers
snacks and a country atmosphere.

Castle Eaton. We could find no traces, not even a ruin, of the castle
which must have stood here once upon a time to give the village its
rather Gothic name. The gardens are full of flowers, and there is a
cool walk under heavily shaded trees from the lychgate to the
church. The latter has a funny little thirteenth-century bell-cote for
the Sanctus bell, and an impressive Norman doorway. Inside you
will find a wall painting of the Madonna in dark red, and the beautifully carved pulpit dates from Tudor times.

Hannington. We liked the look of the *Jolly Tar* pub, which had a
cheerful sign of a sailor with his parrot. You can see Hannington

Hall through the trees as you climb the hill to **Highworth**. An old hilltop town, the views are lovely from here, and there are fine beech trees and seventeenth-century houses.

Blunsdon Abbey. What a disappointment! We'd imagined beautiful grey buildings and a feeling of religion and the past. What we saw were the grey stone ruins of the abbey, which is now used as a background for selling smart caravans of the 1970s. It's true that everything is beautifully kept, ·the grass trimmed and the impressive ruins are carefully preserved. But oh, what a comedown for what was once a sacred place.

Blunsdon St Andrew. Get over the shock of the abbey-and-caravans and enjoy the views here, they are very beautiful, with parkland and richly wooded country on either side of you as you cycle downhill towards Purton. You can see for miles.

Purton. This is a village no longer but a busy town which looks as if it is growing quickly. Fork left as you cycle up the hill into Purton, and then turn left again into a small side-turning. Here there is a fine Elizabethan house called Purton Manor, fronting on to the lane. It is approached up a flight of curved stone steps and all along the lane is a row of beautiful high box trees which smell aromatic in summertime. Honeysuckle grows over the walls. The box trees edge the path to the church which is surprisingly large and important, and on the plain side. But its arches are decorated with painted designs, hundreds of years old, in geometric patterns of blue, terra cotta, grey and brown. The vicar told us he still has a bill, dating back for centuries, for repainting these arches. It was for £8. 15s.

Restrop House. If you cycle along the Wootton Bassett road, after visiting Purton church, you'll see Restrop House on your right. It's Elizabethan, originally a manor house and now used as a farmhouse. It's set in a walled garden. The house was once the home of the Ashley Coopers, relations of the legendary Bolingbrokes, and that great name is very evident hereabouts. The local pub is called the *Bolingbroke Arms*. Visiting Restrop is by appointment. If you write to Mr T. J. Low who owns the house now, he will show you the house and the gardens. It's a delightful muddle of different periods, with a carved Tudor overmantle in dark oak, showing a cannon as part of a coat of arms – little twisted staircases, huge fireplaces, and some linenfold panelling. The garden was bright with lupins and roses when we visited it.

Cricklade Tour Two

Total distance: 20 miles.
O.S. Map: 157.

Outward Route

Leave Cricklade by the B4040 in the Minety direction, and after cycling 1½ miles turn right for **Ashton Keynes**. Continue on the same unclassified road out of Ashton Keynes, turning left after **Northend** for **Somerford Keynes**. Cycle through Poole Keynes, taking the road for **Oaksey** and **Upper Minety**. Continue through the village, to rejoin the B4040 at **Minety**.

Homeward Route

Leave Minety on the B4040 in the Cricklade direction, and after two miles turn left on to unclassified road in Ashton Keynes direction. Turn right after 1½ miles for **Lower Waterhay**. Continue, taking left fork for **Upper Waterhay**, crossing the B4040 and turning left after half a mile for Cricklade, crossing the old canal.

Ashton Keynes is a village near the source of the Thames, crossed by little bridges. The Cotswold Community have settled here – they are a group of people who live together earning no wages and supporting themselves with a farm, cattle, their own hospital. We saw the settlement from the road and it looked a pleasing place, one where unworldly people would be very happy. There was once a great monastery at Ashton just by the church. All that's left is the moat (filled with grass and buttercups) surrounding a farm and some of the fields. One of the barns dates from the Middle Ages – you will see it as you cycle past.

Somerford Keynes. There are man-made lakes near here, and you may be lucky enough to see a water-bird – we saw a heron flying overhead and a V formation of geese – probably from Slimbridge. There's a nice inn with roses round the door called the *Baker's Arms*, and a Tudor manor house which is quite marvellous, with an atmosphere surrounding it which seems still to belong to Shakespeare's time. If you are cycling in this part of the world at daffodil time, you may be lucky enough to hit a day when you can visit the grounds which also has a lovely collection of many gorgeous flowering cherry trees.

We visited the church next door to the manor – we were interested in finding a carved Saxon stone which may have been part of a Viking tomb. We found some carved stones on a windowsill in the church, next to the blocked-up Saxon doorway which is tiny, narrow, and was used by men a thousand years ago. The stones were very ancient and defaced but elaborately carved in patterns similar to Celtic gravestones.

Oaksey. You won't be able to miss the reason why this village is called by its sweet-sounding country name. Everywhere in the district are the magnificent oak trees which stand like guardians in the fields and along the edges of the lanes. The country is richly wooded, and you turn left into the B4040 just at the beginning of **Minety Common**. If you want to have a picnic, continue straight across the main road on to the common for a peaceful and rural setting for your lunch.

Ashton Keynes. Old Father Thames begins his famous journey 'down to the mighty sea' not far from this little place, due south of Coates and north of Kemble. The river here at Ashton is only a few feet wide, crossed by small bridges.

Cricklade Tour Three

Total distance: 25 miles.
O.S. Map: 157.

Outward Route

Leave Cricklade on the B4040 in the direction of Malmesbury. Turn left at **Minety** on to the unclassified road signposted for **Brinkworth**. Turn right on to the B4042 into Brinkworth. In the centre of the village turn left on to unclassified road for **Grittenham** and **Tockenham Wick**. When you meet the A420, turn left for **Wootton Bassett** along this road. Cycle through Wootton Bassett, going straight across the crossroads on to the B4041 for **Hook**. In Hook, turn right on to unclassified road for **Lydiard Tregoze**.

Homeward Route

Leaving Lydiard Tregoze, cycle in the same direction for **Lydiard Millicent** and **Purton**, where you rejoin the B4041 back into Cricklade.

Brinkworth. The road is straight but the surface is a bit uneven as you cycle along the route to Brinkworth. The views to the left are very fine, you can see for miles into a misty distance, and the district's magnificent oaks flourish here. Brinkworth has an interesting little church, Perpendicular in style, with a battlemented tower. You will see the faint traces of wall paintings, and a carved Jacobean pulpit. There are two squints – those curious little openings cut in the chancel arch of a church so that people attending the service sitting behind the arch could see the priest at the altar. They are so narow that one wonders whether the worshippers took it in turn to 'have a squint'. But it does show a strong feeling of concern for the congregation.

Wootton Bassett. Look for the little beamed Town Hall, like a small antique box set on stone pillars. It's early eighteenth century and rather comical. Underneath it we saw an ancient hand-propelled fire engine and – even more astounding to our twentieth-century eyes – a pair of stocks. The holes for the legs were large enough for the stoutest Cotswold farmer! This is an interesting town for those who love antique shops.

Lydiard Tregoze. The 'must' on this trip is Lydiard Tregoze. The manor and the church are both marvels, and worth cycling to even on a wet day. You will cycle through wooded undulating parkland and must turn into a drive which is marked 'Private'. But below the notice are the opening times of Lydiard Park and its church.

We visited the house first. It seems an irony that this beautiful place, a Georgian mansion of supreme elegance, was entirely saved by Swindon Corporation – obviously a town which cares for its treasures. When they bought it, it was a wreck. Now it is so stunningly well-kept that one imagines the noble family who lived there are still around, perhaps walking in their park with its spreading cedars or drinking hot chocolate in their library. The state rooms are filled with paintings and antique furniture – in the dining-room a meal is laid as if the family were expected back to dinner. The elaborate ceilings in the ballroom are rococo, wreathed in garlands. Our most favourite treasure, in a small anteroom to the ballroom, was a marvellous seventeenth-century window. It is Flemish stained glass, patterned with birds, bears, flowers, elephants and hippos.

We then visited the Church of St Mary which, literally, adjoins the manor. John Aubrey, the seventeenth-century diarist, went into raptures over this church, saying: 'It exceeds all churches in this countie'. We agreed. It is just *because* the church has always been remote from the Parish, and because the manor fell into disrepair, that the church has stayed so unaltered. It seems more like the private chapel of a patrician family – you feel you've stepped back two or three hundred years.

The St John family, who came from Normandy with William the Conqueror, owned Lydiard for five hundred years. Their memorials in the church are amazing. On the left of the chancel, don't miss the St John Triptych. It's two hinged screens, the outsides painted in sombre colours with an elaborate family tree. Inside you'll see the handsome Sir John, 1594, in armour, with his wife Lucy and his son Sir John, *his* wife Lady St John (1615) and six Tudor sisters.

There is also a dramatic life-sized golden statue of Edward, a cavalier who died of wounds in the Civil War; the statue has been named 'The Golden Cavalier'. And on the right of the chancel are other marvellous monuments, including one of Sir John with his two wives (one has a baby in her arms) and a fierce-looking Tudor effigy of Nicholas with his wife wearing the fashionable Paris veil. We could write about this chapel for paragraphs, but can't leave out the communion rails. They are wrought iron, gilden with the St John crest and monogram, and the design is so beautiful that it looks as if it is made of golden lace.

Malmesbury

It is a hilltop town on the Bristol Avon, a small, attractive place with narrow, hilly streets. It's famous for its abbey – now partly ruined. The very name of the town is derived from the man who is supposed to have founded the abbey – Maldulph. The abbey became eminent in the ninth century, and grew in prosperity and fame for several hundred years. It's still very beautiful although only part of it remains. There are fascinating carvings of the twelve apostles on either side of the main entrance, very strong and almost modern in style, Henry Moore's style but 800 years ago. There's an elaborately patterned doorway with swans, animals and fishes. But the abbey stone is in bad repair which – with such precious carvings – is regrettable.

There are a number of ancient houses in Malmesbury, and a little carved Market Cross. The *Old Bell* hotel, by the abbey, is striking. It was built in Tudor times, but one massive wall is the remains of the *twelfth-century* castle built next to the abbey 'to annoy the monks' as they say in the town. The *Old Bell* claims to have a ghost, a grey lady whose skeleton was found entombed in one of the walls. The ghost is supposed to slip from the inn to an old burial ground through a gap in the privet hedge and the privet refuses to grow where she passes.

Tours from Malmesbury

Malmesbury Tour One

**Total distance: 29 miles.
O.S. Map: 157.**

Outward Route

Leave Malmesbury on the B4040 in the direction of **Easton Grey** and **Sherston**, forking right after 1½ miles for **Shipton Moyne** (unclassified road). Continue cycling on this unclassified road until you turn right into the A433 for **Tetbury**.

Leave Tetbury by the B4067, in the Cirencester direction, carrying straight across the A433 for **Cherington** (unclassified road). Cycle through Cherington, taking the right fork for **Rodmarton**. After one mile this unclassified road turns left, for two miles, to the village of **Rodmarton**.

Homeward Route

Cycle from Rodmarton south, turning right into the A433 for one mile, then fork left for **Culkerton**, then left again to **Ashley** and **Crudwell**. Cycle through Crudwell to **Eastcourt** on the unclassified road, turning right and left after one mile for **Hankerton**. Follow the same road down to **Charlton** where you rejoin the B4040 back into Malmesbury.

When you start this route, your road takes you through a gently rolling landscape, with wheatfields on either side of the road, and high grass verges which are studded in summertime with the white flowers of Lady's Lace.

Shipton Moyne. We liked the look of the inn, which is called *The Cat and Custard Pot*. There's an inn sign swinging outside showing a lovely cat with his face right inside a pot of custard. On the other side of the sign is a hunting scene with the odd title 'The Kill on Cat and Custard Pot Day'. As this is very much a hunting country, we suppose that a Meet starts from here each year. The church has a fine blue clock, very handsome and dated 1887, and in the churchyard

Old Cottages at Tetbury

was one of the nicest memorials to three people in a family, a lovely laburnum tree in full bloom.

Tetbury is a town which is definitely proud of itself, it's well kept and well heeled. The market hall is Elizabethan and stands on three rows of ancient pillars; it has recently been very well painted. There is an elegant hotel called *The Snooty Fox* which is connected with the Mayfair restaurant of the same name. Its ambience is pleasantly Victorian and the food is not too expensive, but alas! no snacks.

Cherington. The road winds along past farms, and the gardens of the stone houses were spiked with irises and foxgloves. Cherington church has a Norman font and a doorway with a carved stone which seems to represent two beasts shaking paws. The roof is supported by beams on stone corbels, carved with bishops, queens and kings – like a chess game.

The road to the next village of Rodmarton is perfect for cycling, peaceful but interesting with varied scenery all the way.

Rodmarton. There is a little green in front of the church, which has a witch's hat steeple. The village is famous for the two Lysons brothers who lived here. They edited a great work in the early nineteenth century which was called Magna Britannica. It was never finished, which is a tragedy for scholars, for it was going to cover the historic treasures of every county of England at that date (1834 onwards). One of the brothers, Samuel, went to London and became Chief of Records at the Tower, making many etchings of buildings, statues and monuments in Gloucestershire which were published as a collection of Antiquities. He also discovered the Roman settlement at Woodchester, and a mosaic of Orpheus, and spent 25 years preparing coloured drawings of Roman antiquities found in England. There are two Roman roads near Rodmarton, and the remains of a Roman villa. And ploughmen of the past often ploughed up brass and silver coins, without knowing what they were.

We were very interested in the Lysons brothers and tried to find where their house was and whether there was a museum of any kind which showed their drawings and paintings. But nobody seems to know anything about this. Shouldn't Rodmarton do something to commemorate these two gifted people?

Charlton. There's a nice inn here, called the *Horse and Groom*, in the centre of the village, which has a number of gabled houses. Charlton Park is a Jacobean mansion which has been modernised. The poet Dryden lived here, to avoid the plague which was followed by the Great Fire of London.

Malmesbury Tour Two

Total distance: 17 miles.
O.S. Map: 157.

Outward Route

Leave Malmesbury on the B4042 in the direction of **Brinkworth** and **Wootton Bassett**. After three miles turn right in **Little Somerford**. and almost immediately right again for **Great Somerford**. Turn left out of Great Somerford for **Dauntsey**, cycling along the edge of Dauntsey Park (unclassified roads). Continue on the same road until you turn right on to the A420 for **Christian Malford** and **Sutton Benger**.

Homeward Route

Turn right in Sutton Benger on to unclassified road running north towards Malmesbury, passing through **Upper Seagry**, **Startley** and **Rodbourne** until you join the A429 back into Malmesbury.

Little Somerford. The fifteenth-century church is a small gem, which was what its window looks like; as you open the church door, there's a blue window shining exactly opposite you, low and curved and coloured like a moonstone. There is a fascinating piece of unfamiliar history on the wall of the church: a coat of arms of Queen Elizabeth I which shows, not the unicorn facing the lion but a dragon. He has a curly tail and his back is spiked like an iguana's. The Jacobean pulpit is beautifully-carved dark oak, the panels are divided by tall carved thistles. The village of Somerford has stone-porched houses and is very attractive indeed.

Great Somerford. Look for West Street Farm, which has chevron moulding, a shield with a lion and flower-decorated medallions on its walls – they came from an ancient church.

Dauntsey. We were very anxious to see the Doom painting, having never seen one and heard that Dauntsey's was particularly exciting. Unfortunately it is now so old and cracked, and time has faded or darkened its colours so much, that it no longer works as a reminder of hellfire. The demons themselves are not scarlet enough, and both the damned and the blessed are rather hard to sort out! But go and see it, for it is a rarity you won't find in many places. Near the church – rather too near – is a modern house of startling red brick which gave us a slight shock in this gentle Cotswold country of grey and soft gold stone houses.

Christian Malford. The church has two interesting old screens, and a carved font of Norman times. One is inclined to wonder why the fonts were so large – surely babies were smaller, not bigger, in those days? But it seems that many people were christened as adults, so the fonts are large and very imposing in all the old churches one visits.

Sutton Benger. A touch of elegance is sometimes very welcome before setting off for home, and certainly the *Bell House Hotel* here can give you just that. It's a beautifully furnished and decorated place with fine antiques, gardens, an antique shop and very pleasant rooms. A delightful place for half an hour's rest and refreshment.

Malmesbury Tour Three

Total distance: 23 miles.
O.S. Map: 156.

Outward Route

Leave Malmesbury on the B4040 in the direction of **Easton Grey** and **Sherston**, forking left after $\frac{1}{4}$ mile on unclassified road for **Foxley**, running parallel to the river Avon, and eventually cycling by the grounds of **Pinkney Park**. Continue cycling on this unclassified road past a quarry. Turn left to join the B4040 into **Luckington**. Cycle through Luckington and then fork right on to unclassified road to **Great Badminton**.

Homeward Route

Turn right in Great Badminton to cycle along edge of Deer Park to **Little Badminton**, continuing on same road until you turn right on to A433 to **Didmarton**. Turn right on to unclassified road for **Sopworth**. Cycle through Sopworth then turn left for Sherston, joining the B4040 and cycling through Easton Grey and home to Malmesbury.

Sherston. This stone-built village is very pleasing, and the church has some interesting tombs. Look for the *Rattlebone Inn* – its odd name comes from a hero who lived here long ago, and fought for the Danes.

Before you choose this trip for a day of Cotswold cycling, you may decide whether you'd like to go on a date when some of the local gardens around here are open to the public. This is several times a year and is a very pleasant way of varying a cycle tour. **Easton Grey House** opens its garden to the public sometimes. The house is eighteenth century, and you will see bulbs, borders of varied flowers, shrubs and lovely roses. The river Avon flows nearby, and a church tower rises in the distance.

Luckington, which comes next on your route, is another village where there's a gem of a garden to be seen if your visit is timed right. The village itself is quiet and unexceptional, but **Luckington Court** is a beautiful place. You can visit the house and garden on any Bank Holiday or by written appointment to the Honourable Mrs Trevor Horn. Do go. The garden is quite lovely. We saw a very rare hedge, which alternated copper beech and holly, growing together in a pattern of green and bronze leaves. And there are rich herbacious borders as a setting to the Queen Anne house, with a dragon over the roof and a croquet lawn good enough for Alice in Wonderland and her flamingoes.

Great Badminton. It's where those famous Horse Trials take place every year, and it has been the home of the Dukes of Beaufort since the seventeenth century. You can visit Badminton House any Wednesday between May 31 and September 6 in the afternoon. You'll see the Hunt kennels, have tea in the Orangery, and visit the house which is Palladian, huge and grey, with the Beaufort flag flying, and full of an abundance of treasures including paintings of Italian, Dutch and French schools, carving, and lovely furniture. The fields near the house seemed to us to be full of hunters, and the village of houses we thought of as 'retainers' dwellings' since there were important coats of arms over every doorway. Have a look at the Keeper's Lodge if you visit Badminton House; it's a little castle-type building, a sort of folly.

Didmarton. This is a very pleasant village but the road is extremely busy. We were in search of St Laurence's holy well. The saint blessed this well at Didmarton and promised the villagers it would never run dry. It didn't for hundreds of years. We called in at a friendly pub, and an elderly local inhabitant told us where to find the well. Alas, it's bricked up and the pump handle is rusty. It seemed sad to think how once this had been the gathering place of so many Cotswold folk, and a well blessed by their very own saint.

Near the crossroads just beyond the village is a place called Petty France – it was given this name because there was a camp of French prisoners of war here after the Napoleonic wars.

The road home is very pleasant, a thoroughly good road for cycling, over a three-span bridge, rolling fields and, if you're lucky, goldfinches flying out of the hedges just ahead of you. The road is lonely and quiet, too.

Malmesbury Tour Four

Total distance: 24 miles.
O.S. Map: 156.

Outward Route

Take the B4040 in the direction of **Easton Grey**, forking left after
¼ mile for **Foxley**. Turn left in Foxley for Norton, and turn left
again at **Norton** for New Town. Turn right at the crossroads for
Grittleton, cycling through the village until you turn right into the
B4039 for Burton. Return by the same road (B4039) to **Castle
Combe**.

Homeward Route

Leave Castle Combe in the Chippenham direction on the B4039 for
Yatton Keynell. After 1½ miles turn left on to unclassified road for
Kington St Michael. Cycle through Kington and turn right for
Stanton St Quinton and **Lower Stanton St Quinton**, where you cycle
left into the A429 back on the main road to Malmesbury.

Burton. It's a long spread-out village with a particularly pleasant
pub with the nostalgic name of *The Old House at Home*. Inn signs
are always best if they have a different painting on either side, and
this one shows a soldier in a beret, remembering his old Cotswold
home in dreams when he's away at the wars. On the other side of
the sign is an old countryman, hobbling to his village home with a
stick. The pub's licensee, with the same name as her village (she's a
Mrs Burton) made us welcome in the Tally Ho bar. You can get
morning coffee, good snacks and hot food. This is a hunting country
and the chintzes were patterned with hunting scenes, and there was
a stuffed fox, wearing a dog collar and lead, looking at us from a
shelf!

Castle Combe. It is very small and perfect and has a reputation to
live up to. For many people it is their dream of what a village should
be. The river (the By brook) flows fast down the main street, with flat
bridges, pack bridges, and river walks. The houses and shops stand

in a row of golden stone, with a thickly-wooded hill behind them. The village looks almost as if it is a painted backcloth for an old-fashioned production of Shakespeare. Visit the church, which has a little one-sided steeple, and have a look at the cross in the centre of the village, an ancient carved monument which we thought looked Saxon, with elaborate runic carving.

There's an interesting inn, in Cotswold stone of course, which is part of the village architecture; this is the *Castle Hotel*, where they serve hot snacks in the Cellar Bar. You'll enjoy this bar, which has flagstones and fine vaulting, and lots of historic atmosphere to match.

Kington St Michael. The almshouses here are seventeenth century, and at Priory Farm (suitably named) there are the remains of an ancient nunnery. The village is growing into a small new town with good-style cottages in local stone. Perhaps it will not appeal to the cyclist looking for the romantic past. We stopped at the *Jolly Huntsman*, an old inn modernised, originally a building of stone and pink brick. We lunched among the Army and local farm workers in a friendly atmosphere. The pâté with hot toast was a good choice, also 'Huntsman's Lunch' – cheddar cheese, rolls and pickles. Very reasonably priced.

Yatton Keynell. The hamlet is turning into a 'new' village and in some ways has lost its character, but there are some stone-built farms, a thatched dovecote, and dry stone walls, forming a background to a magnificent copper beach. But the place is still growing, and the small intimacy of the past is gone.

Stanton St Quinton. You approach the village by a narrow lane with high hedges. This is pleasant cycling country and in summer there is meadowsweet, rose-bay willowherb and scarlet poppies. We went *under* the motorway to get to Stanton, a curious sensation! The village has stone walls, abundant roses and roofs covered in flowering lichen. We visited the church. Its lychgate had carved angel faces as you enter from the road, and it's worth walking all round the outside of the church. It often happens that you'll find some curious or rare carving on the outer walls of these ancient buildings. At Stanton we found a marvellous sculpture of Christ, almost Henry Moore style, standing on a dragon which must have represented the devil. The church has a delicate arched balustrade all round the roof.

Moreton-in-Marsh

Many people believe the name of this Cotswold town doesn't refer to a marsh at all but to a march, that is to say a boundary. But whether it is the boundary between Gloucestershire and Oxfordshire, or that infinitely older one between Wessex and Mercia, is unknown. The name could refer to ancient flooding. It could even be a pun.

The wide main street is, in actual fact, the Fosse Way but it has been built up and there's no longer any danger of floods here. At one end of the village you will see Redesdale Hall, presented to the local council twenty years ago by Lord Dulverton. Opposite is a curious little tower with a seventeenth-century clock and bell, once used as a lock-up.

Charles I stayed the night at Moreton during the Civil War and slept at the *White Hart Inn*. Another old inn which is very much worth a visit was once the manor house, and has a secret passage which used to run underground to the church. But why, we wondered?

There is a new church, built in Victorian times, on the site of an older (and doubtless more beautiful) one and made from its stones. In the churchyard is a holy well which has been covered in. There are very attractive shops in Moreton, including interesting antique shops.

Two miles east of Moreton is the elegant Four Shire Stone which is now, because of boundary adjustings, the *three* shire stone. It is the meeting-place of Gloucestershire, Oxfordshire and Warwickshire.

Tours from Moreton-in-Marsh

Moreton-in-Marsh Tour One

Total distance: 20 miles.
O.S. Map: 144.

Outward Route

Take the A429 (Fosse Way) turning left after four miles to **Stretton on Fosse**. Continue through Stretton to join the B4479, turning left for **Paxford**. Cycle on the B4479 past Northwick Park to **Blockley**. Continue on the same road until you meet the A44, then turn left into this road for half a mile. Then turn right on to an unclassified road for **Sezincote** (there are details of how to get there exactly in our description of this place).

Homeward Route

Cycle on the same unclassified road in the same direction out of **Sezincote** for one mile, then turn left for **Longborough**. Continue until you meet the A429, then turn right into it. Cycle two miles, then turn left for **Broadwell**. Return on the A429 to Moreton-in-Marsh.

Blockley, in the north Cotswolds, is large and rather built up, with new as well as old houses. The real old village is on a hill. There was a Bishop's Palace just by the church; a manor house is there now. We specially wanted to see the Rushout chapel in the church, as we'd heard about the memorials to this family. The chapel (which the Rushouts had built for themselves in the church) is curious. It's raised three feet above the rest of the church, and we climbed up a pew to get into it. The vicar told us that when the chapel was built, a charnel house was discovered below, containing over 2,000 skulls!

It seems that in medieval times Blockley was one of the few consecrated grounds for miles around where people were allowed to bury their dead. They had to bring the coffins the day before burial to a house near the church, called 'Porch House', where the coffin was left overnight in the porch. Later on, of course, other churches were built and Blockley no longer had this gruesome privilege; but all those skulls are under the Rushout chapel floor.

The Rushouts themselves can be seen in a collection of marble busts; they're impressive but somehow arrogant, with high-bridged noses and haughty faces. Elizabeth, who became Countess of Northampton and who looks like Mrs Siddons, must have had a charitable (or patronising?) heart, since she left a permanent bequest for loaves of bread to be stacked in the pews here at Blockley every other Sunday. The custom actually continued into the 1920s, when the loaves were simply left around by the parishioners. The vicar remarked: 'Nobody was really in need of bread'. There was a fine chained Bible in the church; and the most pathetic memorial to the Rushouts was to little Caroline, only 8, who died in 1878 and who looked just like Alice in Wonderland.

In the corner of the Rushout chapel we found another tomb, a Tudor one with two figures in ruffs. Their name was Childe and they preceded the Rushouts. A memorial says happily:

'Return to thy rest O my Sole
For the lord hath dealth bountifully with thee.'

Note after visiting Blockley. If you happen to be in this area in May or October, you might like to visit **Batsford Park** which is 1½ miles north-west of Moreton and a mile south as you come from Blockley on to the A44. These are large gardens with flowering cherries, many rare trees, and bulbs in springtime, and over 900 named varieties of trees and shrubs – a real treasury for the garden lover.

Before you cycle to Sezincote, if you want lunch or a drink the *Horse & Groom* at Bourton-on-the-Hill, a little further on the A44 in the Moreton direction, is smart. The village is attractive with blue hills in the distance.

Sezincote will take a bit of finding – we lost ourselves once. If you cycle along the road in the Longborough direction for about 1½ miles you'll see a road marked 'Private' on the left. It leads towards a farm where you must turn left. This is an estate of houses and farm, its quite acceptable to cycle there – we obtained permission from one of the houses. It's certainly worth the trip; the little road runs along the back of a most astonishing house – a rococo mansion built by Sir Charles Cockerell of the East India Company. It's in the Moorish style with minarets and onion-shaped domes, and it's exactly like the Brighton Pavilion only smaller. It was built, in fact, *before* the Pavilion. The Prince Regent saw it and was so entranced by its rather àbsurd beauty that he copied it in Brighton. It's extraordinary to see the shape of this fantastic mansion in the middle of English woods and surrounded by farms.

Longborough. A pretty and quiet village in a dip, with fine views and gardens full of pink Queen Elizabeth roses and hollyhocks in summer. The pinnacled church has a square tower and can be seen over a stone wall as you cycle along the pleasant road.

Broadwell. There are panoramic views round here, they stretch away like an Elizabethan wall painting, so beautiful as to seem almost artificial. There's a big village green, with willows for shade and grass to sit on while you picnic. A row of high firs grows by the walls of a beautiful Elizabethan house.

Moreton-in-Marsh Tour Two

Total distance: 21 miles.
O.S. Maps: 144, 145.

Outward Route

Leave Moreton-in-Marsh on a north-easterly route for **Todenham**, turning right for **Great Wolford**. Continue on same road, crossing Stanford Brook to **Barton-on-the-Heath**. Turn left for **Long Compton Mill**, **Harrow Hill**, where you branch left for **Whichford**, with Wychford Woods on your right. Turn left in Whichford and left again almost immediately in the direction of **Lower Brailes**. Then turn left for **Sutton-under-Brailes**.

Homeward Route

Turn left for **Stourton** and **Cherington**, crossing the A34 to **Little Wolford** and rejoining the outward route at **Great Wolford**, home to Moreton.

Todenham. This pleasant village has a row of stone cottages and a manor house. It's interesting that the church is named after St Thomas à Becket. His murder seems to crop up over and over again in this part of the world; it was a Tracey of the Cotswolds who was one of the five knights who killed our English saint. We liked the brass, quite small but very clear, commemorating William Molton and his wife Millicent. They are both in Tudor dress, and a little poem says piously:

> 'Stay Passenger, this Tomb doth Hould
> A Coffin Full of Holy Mould.'

They kneel, oddly enough, on either side of a coffin which we suppose is their own? The date of the brass is 1604.

Great Wolford. It's hilly round here and the road hasn't such a good surface as many little unclassified Cotswold roads. But the great oaks and long views give the impression that you are cycling through parkland, with a spire in the distance sometimes and not a soul in sight. The village is full of golden stone houses and there's a school house and a farm by the church. Standing back from the road is the *Fox & Hounds* pub which looks cosy and cared for.

Barton-on-the-Heath. The road to Barton is winding, with oaks on either side. The village is minute, with a big Elizabethan house and a church up stone steps placed in grass. The one curious thing we found in the ancient, simple church was a little fat piggy animal with a snout and a curly tail. He was carved in stone on the inside of the chancel arch and must have been one of a frieze of cheerful medieval creatures. He is the last, but still frolicking 700 years later. As you cycle out of Barton you'll pass Barton House, a magnificent Tudor building, quite perfect, standing a little way back from its open gates.

Sutton-under-Brailes. The road meanders through pastures, with ash and elm trees on either side. Someone has brought an old tithe barn to life again with hanging baskets of flowers suspended in its huge doors. The cottage gardens are also full of flowers in summer, and it's a happy place to cycle through.

Cherington. The pastures are rich and there are plentiful cattle grazing, small cottages and a manor or two. Don't miss the church on the Burmington Road. The windows are wonderful. One of them, on the right as you face the altar, is a stained glass montage of fragments which we supposed were once part of a set of medieval windows. The montage had been put together by an artist and contains Elizabethan faces, praying hands, mailed heads, priests, a dark African face, a baby, an angel, a flower. On the left is a window in which both modern and ancient glass are combined – a scene of Thomas à Beckett's murder is surrounded by faint, lovely butterflies, beasts and Cotswold birds.

Little Wolford. Cycle along the curving road under some of the country's magnificent oaks. The fields stretch away on either side, and you pass an ancient barn and climb a gentle hill to another farming village, with views of the distant hills.

The Porch, Northleach Church

Northleach

These days, the town is really a dormitory for the motor industry of Witney. But it hasn't been spoiled, and still keeps its wide street and traditional houses, just as when it was part of the great wool trade, supplying the best fleeces in Europe.

The wool church has a fascinating and most elaborate porch with six carved pinnacles. The porch has an upper room which can be reached by a staircase up one of the turrets. The brasses in Northleach's church are marvellous and really do give an idea of what those rich wool merchants actually looked like. You'll notice that a lot of the figures seem to have a sheep somewhere in the design – sheep meant money to Northleach folk.

There's an old joke about the town because in the past it was dominated by three buildings, a prison at one end of the village as it used to be (it's supposed to have a treadmill there still), the church in the middle, and the workhouse at the other end of the village. The joke describes Northleach as 'Damnation – Salvation – Starvation'.

The river Leach, which gives the town its name, is a minute stream here, flowing in little more than a ditch. But the town has charm. There are corners where the Tudor houses have overhanging storeys projecting almost four feet, an old Wool House restaurant which looks attractive, and many of the oldest houses are timbered.

109

Tours from Northleach

Northleach Tour One

Total distance: 15 miles.
O.S. Map: 144.

Outward Route

Take Fosse Way (A429) in Cirencester direction for half a mile then
turn right for **Yanworth**. Fork left in Yanworth to come to the river
Coln. Push bike through woodland path alongside river to site of
Roman Temple; through Chedworth Woods to site of Roman Villa.
Continue past Tumulus (left) with Withington Woods on left,
forking left for **Cassey Compton** to Withington.

Homeward Route

Turn right in **Withington**, crossing old railway track and cycle on steep
downhill gradient to **Compton Abdale**. Turn left for ¾ mile and cross
A40 for **Hazleton**. Turn right down steep hill for **Hampnett** (remains
of Cross on right). Back through Prison Copse to Northleach.

Yanworth. You cycle along the wonderful, arrow-straight Roman
Road, the Fosse Way, in the direction of Cirencester and turn off
right for Yanworth. This is where the Chedworth Roman villa is to
be found on the edge of the Chedworth Woods.

Roman Villa. (Also covered in Cirencester Tour Three.) It's a National Trust site and the form of the villa can be clearly seen. It was
built in A.D. 200 when the Romans were well and truly established
in Britain, and the house belonged, not to Romans themselves, but
to Britons who'd become 'Romanised'. The people who lived here
led a civilised life, as you'll see easily from this beautifully designed
house, with its reception rooms, decorated floors, Sauna and Turkish-
type baths. There is also a small museum with more Roman treasures
to be studied. This is one of the best Roman sites we've ever visited,
and its position, with the thick woods nearby and meadows like
those in a park stretching down to the valley, make it a perfect choice
for a cycle ride.

Cassey Compton. The village is on the river Coln, and here you'll see the beautiful manor of Cassey Compton. It was built by Sir Richard Howe in the early 1600s in the shape of an L, with a moat and drawbridge. It's a farm now, and local people say it is haunted.

Compton Abdale. In the distance at a curve in the road it looks just like a toy village built by children. There's a manor house with dovecotes in its walls, a big grey barn and – as we passed by – a family on the manor lawns were having tea. In the village, too, there's the remains of an old stone windmill. The whole effect is of dreamy yesterday. The church is small and well proportioned, at the end of a lane, and the views of woods and valleys are beautiful. We passed many cottages with staddle stones, on the edge of a swift-flowing stream, and the farms are well kept and industrious-looking.

The road continues between wooded hills, with Compton Grove on your left, and from here you cycle down into Withington and Chedworth Woods. We liked this part of the country *very* much.

Withington. There are newly-built rather smart houses here; built of local stone interspersed among the old stone-walled cottages of the old village. The *Mill Inn* and the *Mill House* are both elegant eating places, one on either side of the Coln river. The *Mill House* is fourteenth-century and was a cornmill until recently. The waggoners brought their corn here to be ground while they enjoyed a mug of ale. There's a fine old 1588 fireback in the old dining-room at the inn, with a design of two anchors, vines and the fleur-de-lys. And you'll see the water wheel here, and the ovens too, which are immediately beneath the wheel! The church at Withington has a fascinating doorway of zigzag decorations and little beakheads, but the inside of the church is over-restored, alas, and has lost much of its atmosphere.

Hazleton is a gated village. The church is outside the gates, but you'll have to get off your bicycle to open and close the gates which protect cattle grazing on the common. We saw a pheasant family with nine chicks marching down the middle of the road, and the fields were full of well-fed sheep, comfortable-looking as white cushions. The peaceful lane, with views of low hills, has an agricultural air about it. The ride is attractive, if rather steep, but one dip will send you spinning halfway up the next hill if you use your impetus skilfully. Goldfinches fly out of the hedgerows, and wild scabious, poppies and willowherb grow in summertime. This is a country for the lover of wild flowers.

111

Mill Inn, Withington

Hampnett. The road to the village is blue with wild geraniums in midsummer, the hills roll away in the distance, and Hampnett is perched on top of a small hill. The air freshens as you reach the crest. Bright yellow bedstraw grows on top of the churchyard walls. The church is an oddity; a Victorian rector took it into his head to decorate it in the way that churches were painted in medieval times. The chancel is covered with paintings in geometric or flower designs in the old style, red or green, dark brown or black. The effect is curious but charming, and certainly the stone is enhanced by this elaborate, dense decoration, including central figures of angels. Opposite the church on the walls of an old barn, an Albertine rose bloomed, its russet leaves rather the colour of the wall paintings.

112

Northleach Tour Two

Total distance: 10 miles.
O.S. Map: 144.

Outward Route

Join A429 in Stow-on-the-Wold direction, turning left after $\frac{3}{4}$ mile for **Turkdean** and **Notgrove**. Cross B4068 due north and, $1\frac{1}{2}$ miles later, cross A436 following the valley of the Windrush to **Guiting Power**.

Homeward Route

Turn left in Guiting Power for **Hawling Lodge** and **Hawling**, taking left turn in Hawling in **Hazleton** direction, crossing track of old railway with tumulus and earthworks on right at Penn Hill to **Salperton Park**, continuing through **Hampnett** and back to Northleach.

Turkdean. You ride through beechwoods which grow high as a cathedral to this village which has three manor houses and a church with a Norman doorway. We saw beautiful views through gaps in garden hedges. It's a charming small place, very unspoiled.

Notgrove. The road is a smoothly running and level surface with a wealth of blue geraniums in summer. They literally make a solid blue patch like the sky. There's a sloping green, and the village is at the bottom with stone-tiled cottages and a small rise leading to the manor and the church.

Do visit the church, it's special. As well as stone figures of two priests, 1325 and 1390, very mysterious and worn, and a lovely Whittington lady of 1630 with a ruff and veil, there is a touching piece of tapestry-work which hangs as the background to the altar. This is modern. It was embroidered by the Anderson family, three generations of them, and both Anderson women *and* men helped to sew this scene of Notgrove church and countryside. (We suppose that the family must have lived at the manor.) All the embroidery was done between 1936 and 1954 and there are symbols representing various people in the family, embroidered as a border. A girl called Diana is represented by a basket of roses, and Hermione, whose childhood nickname was 'Mink', is represented by two running furry minks. It's good to see a church in which there are *present-day* family treasures as well as things left by devout people hundreds of years ago.

Outside this well looked-after church there's a tiny ancient stone crucifix on the wall with a figure which looks as if it was carved by a child.

And under the yew tree somebody had arranged gravestones in a star pattern all round the tree.

Hawling is a cosy corner. Two manor houses, a little church and a farm huddled together. We'd been told there were a collection of sundials on the church but couldn't find these at all. We did find some small brass plaques of the Stratford family, seventeenth century, well polished, all with the lion coat of arms; they seemed to have inter-married – everybody was related to everybody else! You can sit on the wall by the churchyard, look at the church and the manor, and dream of yesterday.

Old Stocks at Stow-on-the-Wold

Stow-on-the-Wold

Stow, on a ridge between the upper valleys of two rivers, the Windrush and the Evenlode, is a small town just over the borders into Gloucestershire. It's very exposed to wind and weather and there's a local saying which remarks succinctly: 'Stow-on-the-Wold where the wind blows cold'.

Stow first comes into history in 1107, when King Henry I gave it borough status and a Thursday market. The wide main street you see today was the scene of this market, and at times there were many thousands of sheep on sale there, an extraordinary thought as you cycle along it now. A great battle, the last important one in the Civil War, was fought at Stow in 1646. The Royalists were defeated, and many of the prisoners, as was the habit of the Roundheads, were locked in the church.

The focal point of Stow is its enormous market square, built in the form of an enclosure in which to keep the animals on market day. The church, fifteenth century, replaced an older, Norman church. It is typical of the churches built from the profits of the Cotswold woollen industry, beautiful and highly decorated; a clerestory was added in the fifteenth century and the wide chancel arch was restored at that time. When you visit the church, go and look at the painting of the Crucifixion by Gaspard de Craeyer, a seventeenth-century painter who knew Rubens and Van Dyke.

Stow has the usual solid, handsome stone houses – but St Edward's is rather fine, with its thin fluted pillars. It is now partly a museum. In the market place you'll see the old stocks in which our ancestors spent many uncomfortable and angry hours. They are objects which always have a particular fascination – of wonderment at the harshness that people took for granted. Yet those same people wrote poetry and lived in houses infinitely more beautiful than ours.

Tours From Stow-on-the-Wold

Stow-on-the-Wold Tour One

Total distance: 20 miles.
O.S. Map: 144.

Outward Route

Leave Stow on the A429 in a northerly direction (towards Moreton-in-Marsh), cycle through **Donnington** and continue for a further two miles, turning left on an unclassified road for **Longborough**. Take the left fork out of Longborough, and when you meet the A424 turn right and cycle 2½ miles, turning left on to unclassified road for **Hinchwick** and **Condicote**. Fork right out of Condicote, then right again at the next crossing, cycling over Chalk Hill in the direction of Guiting Power. Take third left unclassified road signposted for **Naunton** When you meet the A436, turn left and fork left into Naunton village almost immediately.

Homeward Route

Cycle out of Naunton on same unclassified road, following the Windrush and crossing A436 in Upper Slaughter direction. Turn right at the next T junction and then sharp left almost immediately into the village of Upper Slaughter. Turn left out of Upper Slaughter and cycle on unclassified road to join the A436 and continue on the main road for three miles, turning left into **Lower Swell**. Cycle north out of the village to **Upper Swell**, then turn right to join the B4077 back into Stow.

Longborough. Set in a hollow, this is a pretty village of small cottages and gardens. The distant views are particularly fine.

Condicote. If you are interested in traces of prehistoric times, you will find these near Condicote. There is a tumulus here, one of the ancient burial mounds which still have their mystery, where men buried their dead long before the Romans came to Britain. And at Eubury camp, which is also near here, there is a huge mound, nearly eight acres, now covered with trees, which is also pre-Roman.

We visited the church which has a timbered roof. Roofs of this kind always give you a particular feeling of antiquity; they are

116

oddly warm and homely, and somehow more comfortable than stone, however beautifully carved it is.

Naunton. The hedgerows round here are ideal for the makers of blackberry pie or elderberry wine, both of which fruits are abundant in early autumn. Naunton is a pretty backwater. The village seems to lie both high and low, with the Windrush literally pushing through the valley. Look for the small stone *Black Horse Inn* and the old barn with its dovecote nearby. The beautiful manor house is by the river, and madonna lilies grow near the small church, where you'll find a memorial brass to the man who wrote 'The Cotswold Muse'. He was Clement Barksdale and was rector of this parish in the 1600s, and put up the plate himself!

Upper Slaughter. You must look out for the lovely Elizabethan manor house, one of the finest in the area. It stands at the end of an avenue of trees, and has graceful windows and 15 tall Elizabethan chimneys. We could just imagine Queen Bess staying there on one of her queenly tours of the countryside. The little church is on a steep slope, and the River Eye flows busily by. We saw an interesting sign for the new hotel and restaurant, *The Lords of the Manor*, in an elegant stone courtyard. We searched about for signs of the stronghold where the Saxons hid during the raids of the Danish Vikings but couldn't see this, although it is described as a mound 80 feet across, covered wth trees like a small orchard.

Lower Swell. The country here is one of huge beeches and lonely roads. The old stone walls are velvety with moss. The road rises and falls, but the cycling is very pleasant and the fields spread on either side with no sign of a house. When you arrive at the village you'll see attractive little cottages, a pleasant hotel, *The Old Farm House* with its tempting sign 'Good food and fine cellar'. A stream runs by, facing the hotel – it's the River Dikler. In an ancient smithy both antique and modern ironwork is made, and on the village green stands an elegant Georgian pillar topped by an urn.

Upper Swell. The village is very small, just a handful of houses and a tiny church, a stone bridge, and the river Dikler flowing – really fast. It's just the river to sit by if you feel like a picnic or a cup of coffee from your thermos flask. The church is much restored, but has traces of the thirteenth century, and we liked the old black and white roof with its dark timbers. The church porch has comfortable much-worn stone seats on either side, and a Norman doorway.

Stow-on-the-Wold Tour Two

Total distance: 23 miles.
O.S. Map: 144.

Outward Route

Take the A436 out of Stow in Andoversford/Cheltenham direction, through **Lower Swell** where you fork left on to unclassified road for **Lower Slaughter**. Continue to meet the A429 then turn right and cycle along it for one mile to the left-hand turn for **Bourton-on-the-Water**.

Homeward Route

Continue on the same road for **Little Rissington**. After visiting the village, retrace your route for one mile, turning sharp left on to another unclassified road for **Great Rissington** and **Great Barrington**. Turn left at Great Barrington on unclassified road for **Taynton**. Cycle through the village and turn sharp left on to A424 back home to Stow.

Lower Slaughter. The road is narrow and winding, and suddenly you come to the village which is a little gem. As a matter of fact, it has been painted by scores of artists, and when you see it you'll see why. The river flows in front of the houses, crossed by little stone and wooden bridges, there are clipped yew and box hedges with one growing so close to the house that a hole had to be clipped out for the window behind it to get the daylight. We saw a man roofing a cottage with the thin-cut Cotswold stone tiles which give the houses in this part of the world such a particular charm. The manor, on the river's edge, has a fine croquet lawn which seems just right, and at one of the upstairs windows was a crowd of friendly dolls! Lower Slaughter is pure Cotswold – the marvellous houses, sparkling water, great shady trees, white roses, white doves. And the yews are dark green umbrellas on every riverside lawn.

Bourton-on-the-Water. It's the river's effect on this village which draws crowds of delighted visitors in summertime. There are few

Lower Slaughter

places where water meanders, brimming, under such a number of small stone bridges, right on the main street. There seem to be half a dozen little pack bridges, slightly humped in the middle, crossing and recrossing the Windrush. Sloping lawns edge the river, and graceful trees give shade on fine days along the banks.

When you walk through Bourton you can call in to see a model of the village in the garden of the inn; and look out for an intriguing shop called 'Farmers' which has antiques and bric-a-brac bought from local houses, books and – when we were at Bourton – a collection of old white satin shoes like wedding slippers. You can also buy local pottery and delicious Cotswold honey. At Birdland Zoo Gardens, open every day from 10 to dusk, there are exotic birds and flowers to be seen, a rookery for the delightful penguins everybody loves, and a new tropical house where multicoloured humming birds and other tropical birds can be seen flying free.

Little Rissington. There are three of these villages, and on the signposts they're called 'The Rissingtons' (respectively Wick, Little and Great). Cycling through Little Rissington under high trees, you will

Bourton-on-the-Water

see the houses of matching stone facing the road in simple honey-coloured rows. Even the new houses – and a few are being built – are made of the same stone to blend in with the past.

Great Rissington. Turn at the sign which says 'Village Only'. *The Lamb Inn*, with its sign of a black-faced gambolling lamb, offers accommodation and snacks. The creamy stone houses here are built in tiers down a slope, and there are low hills in the distance. A stunning view of two great houses can be seen at the bottom of the hill near the church which has a sturdy fifteenth-century tower. One of the manors has a row of limes in the garden, 15 feet high, all grown to the same size, neat as well drilled soldiers. Great Rissington is near the Oxfordshire border.

Wick Rissington. Villages looked like this in medieval times – a few cottages and a manor set in the middle of fields – a kind of island. Many of the small houses are thatched and have low 'dry' stone walls. There's a riot of sweet peas in this little place in summer.

Stroud

It is a small, unpretentious, not very historically interesting town; every street seems to go either up or down – Stroud is built on a number of hillsides. For quite a long period it was the heart of the great west of England cloth industry. Stroud had everything needed to make it a success in those times, a damp climate which stopped the yarn from breaking, fast-flowing streams for water power, Fuller's Earth nearby (used in dyeing), and an abundance of teasels, needed to raise the nap of fine quality cloth. Finally, there was a great city as an outlet for Stroud's cloth – Bristol.

In spite of so much prosperity there is not much to show now. The steep streets do give an air of age, but many old houses have been pulled down and replaced by shops and offices. There are few antiquities. The pillared Subscription Rooms are quite charming – they are typically Georgian, just the place where a Jane Austen heroine might have danced a quadrille. The Town Hall is restored sixteenth-century and the Museum and Art school are mainly concerned with the rise of the woollen industry in the region.

There's an Annual Festival, if you are in Stroud in the autumn, of religious drama and the arts. At West Grange, Beeches Green, you can see an amusing collection of old carriages; and Stratford Park, with its lake and cedar trees, is pleasant. Perhaps the most beautiful sights in the area are the picturesque Stroudwater hills which can be seen around the town.

Tours from Stroud

Stroud Tour One

Total distance: 16 miles.
O.S. Maps: 143, 156

Outward Route

Leave Stroud in north-east direction, on A46, turn right almost
immediately on to unclassified road towards **Lypiatt Park**. Cycle
alongside the Park until you reach remains of a partly Saxon Cross,
then turn right for **Bisley**. After visiting Bisley return to the same
unclassified road (*Calf Way*) and cycle north until the road joins the
B4070. After ½ mile turn left at crossroads for **Cranham**, cycling
across Cranham Common. Continue on same unclassified road
along the edge of Buckholt Woods to join the A46, turning left in
Stroud direction. Almost immediately after you join the main road,
turn sharp right for **Prinknash Abbey**.

Homeward Route

Cycle back to the A46, turning right for Stroud direction. Cycle to
Painswick. After visiting Painswick, cycle home on the A46 into
Stroud through the Painswick Valley.

Bisley. If you cycle to the church you will see **Over Court** which is by
the churchyard, a lovely stone house, part of it built in the 1400s.
Queen Elizabeth inherited it and when she became queen is said to
have stayed a night in her manor. In the church, look for the figure
of a knight, his legs are crossed (which means he was a Crusader)
and he is probably a De Bisley. And look at the elaborate font
which has carved fishes swimming inside it. In the churchyard is a
strange six-sided stone structure, a mixture of lantern and cross,
covering a vault which was once a well – it is 700 years old.

Cranham. When you cross the A46 from Cranham you'll come to **Prinknash Park** which is over a hundred acres in extent. The Priory is a beautiful stone abbey where once Henry VIII and Anne Boleyn visited the Abbot of Gloucester, on a hunting trip. Henry's coat of arms can still be seen in some of the Abbey windows. It's one of history's ironies that soon after the Royal visit Henry dissolved the monasteries and Prinknash became the property of the Crown. Now, after many hundreds of years and a stormy history which included quartering of troops here during the Civil War, the monks are back. They came to Prinknash Priory from the Island of Caldy in 1928, and in 1939 the Priory was raised to the status of an Abbey. The monks are now busy building a new Abbey, but the old Priory is very beautiful and can be visited. The chapel has stained glass windows, carved stalls, and the statues of two British saints – Thomas More and Archbishop Fisher.

The Cotswold area has always been noted for its arts and crafts, and when fine clay was discovered on the Prinknash estate, the monks began to make pottery. The first clay was used only for rosaries, but now the famous Prinknash pottery is well established and exported all over the world. The pottery has now been made at Prinknash for nearly 70 years. We liked it very much, particularly the pewter-coloured lustre ware. We bought a silvery tankard, just the right rounded shape for garden roses. The pottery is in about four different colours, all with a distinctive brilliance – there is a range of golden brown, cobalt blue, a yellowish-green and the famous pewter colour.

Painswick. We were fascinated by the marks of the Civil War which can still be seen on Painswick church. The Roundheads hid in the church during one of the battles with the Cavaliers, and you can still see the red marks from flames, and pock-marks from shot, caused when the Royalists tried to smoke them out. The church has an unusual clock painted in scarlet and gold instead of the traditional clock-face blue. In the churchyard are the 99 yews which many people connect with Painswick. Some visitors swear there are a hundred. There is a ceremony at the church in autumn, the children hold hands and walk round the churchyard and a hymn is sung. It's a medieval custom of 'embracing the church'. In the town there is the old Court House where King Charles I stayed, which is open to the public during the summer, and the *Falcon Inn* which has kept its ancient bowling green.

Stroud Tour Two

Total distance: 24 miles.
O.S. Map: 156.

Outward Route

Leave Stroud on the A4096 in the direction of Frampton-on-Severn, turning left after one mile on to the B4066. Cycle through **Stanley Wood** and **Coley Wood** to **Crawley, Uley** and **Woodmancote**. In Woodmancote you join the A4135 for one mile then fork left on to the B4060 for **Stinchcombe, Stancombe Park** (site of Roman Villa) and **North Nibley**. Continue on the B4060 to **Wotton-under-Edge**. The B4060 joins the B4059 on the outskirts of Wotton.

Homeward Route

Continue cycling on the B4058 until it joins the A4135 for **Kingscote**, passing Kingscote Park on your left. Then turn left on to the A46 to Horsley, **Nailsworth** and **Woodchester**, and back to Stroud.

It's a fairly long climb out of Stroud on this trip, but it's worth every push of the cycle wheel, for when you get to the top you are on a crest of downland. The view is superb for miles, with a landscape of Severn valleys, blue distances, trees and that silence of deserted country places, with the wind that always blows when you are on the hills. Then there is a fine winding run and you can freewheel downhill through beechwoods to Uley.

Uley. There are small Georgian houses here, some painted pink. A rich valley of cedars and other large parkland trees spreads around the village and the views of hilly distances are stunning. We liked the look of the eighteenth-century *King's Head*, a most attractive Georgian pub at Uley. This village was once famous for blue woollen cloth, and many of the houses have stone warehouses next door which were used for storing the cloth. We were told that if you want to spend a little time exploring, you can ask locally for the key of a prehistoric camp on Uley Berry, 800 feet up. It has three burial chambers.

A small turning on the left just before the village leads to **Owlpen Manor**. You can visit this lovely manor house if you are here on a Friday afternoon in June or July. It is in Cotswold stone, dated from the fifteenth-century to early eighteenth century. As well as the manor house, there are terraced gardens, old shrub roses and clipped yews to be seen.

Woodmancote. The Market Hall is Georgian, and a stone figure looks down at you from a newly painted blue and white niche. We thought she was Queen Anne, elegant in an elaborate gown. There is an interesting pub in the village called the *Apple Tree Inn*, with two bars, both in the rustic style and just right for a refreshing glass of cider.

As we left the village we noticed many fine horses in the meadows, including a white mare with a coal black foal. The panoramic views on this route continue all the way until you cycle into Wotton.

Wotton-under-Edge. The town is rather crowded and trafficky, with a one-way street system, but it still has a certain charm and historic interest. The gables and timbered almshouses were built in 1632, and Katharine Lady Berkeley founded the grammar school in Long Street in 1384. The buildings are not as old as this but they are still ancient and beautiful. Wotton, like Uley, was a weaving centre, and every cottage used to have a spindle or a loom. A famous man who was destined to change people's lives, not at spinning but in offices, lived here in Orchard Street. He was Isaac Pitman, the inventor of shorthand.

There are many pleasant places to lunch, including the *Ram*, by the brook, *The Swan* in Market Street, or there's the *Sherman's Arms* where the road is as high as the bedrooms and there are antique bars below the level of the street.

Kingscote. On the outskirts of this village you come to Ashel Barn (known as the Chestles). It was once a Roman outpost and Roman coins and flint arrowheads have been found here. An old coffin made of stone was also discovered when a farmer was ploughing his field.

In the porch of the church, look for a brass tablet to Doctor Jenner (who was educated at Wotton's old grammar school). He was the pioneer of vaccination against smallpox and he married a Kingscote of Kingscote. The oak screen in the church is Jacobean, very beautifully carved. One of the stained glass windows shows a picture of Sir Galahad.

Nailsworth. Beautifully situated in a valley of marvellous beechwoods, the village had a famous glassworks in Tudor and Stuart days. The name 'Nailsworth glass' is still given to the candy-striped whorled glass in white or bright colours which is a favourite of collectors. In the ruins of the old glassworks two small glass boots were once found. The village has attractive old houses and mills, and behind it is the Nailsworth Ladder, a chalk hill rising steeply with a gradient of 1 in 3½ and used for car trials. W. H. Davies, the tramp poet, died at Nailsworth in 1940. One of his most loved poems exactly suits this part of the Cotswolds and a cyclist's view of it.

> 'What is life, if, full of care
> We have no time to stand and stare?
> No time to stand beneath the boughs
> And stare as long as sheep or cows:
> No time to see, when woods we pass,
> Where squirrels hide their nuts in grass.'

Witney

This town is perhaps the nearest thing to an industrially-based town you'll see in this part of the Cotswolds. It's built on rather low-lying ground around the Windrush and its name comes from an island – Watta's Island – which stood among what were then the Windrush marshes.

Witney has been famous for making beautiful blankets for hundreds of years; this success was due to two things which worked so well together – Cotswold wool and Windrush water. The fine local sheep supplied the wool and the river water was also considered important. In a seventeenth-century history of Oxfordshire, the writer Doctor Plot commented that the Windrush water ensured 'that no place yields blanketing so notoriously white as is made at Witney'. It reads rather like a modern advertisement! After the decline in importance of Cotswold wool, Witney went on being successful because the town was imaginative at selling its blankets, especially to the North American Indians via the Hudson Bay Company. And even today – by concentrating on quality – the weavers of Witney are famous.

The money from this success at making blankets hundreds of years ago has left its traces in interesting Witney antiquities. There's the old Blanket Hall. And the Butter Cross, an odd little Jacobean building with a clock on top where presumably butter used to be sold. The town hall is tiny, built of stone and standing on pillars; it has a one-handed clock. If you're interested to see some portraits of a Witney family who made blankets in Jacobean times, there are some good 'wool' brasses in the high-spired church.

But perhaps the most striking feature of all, when you cycle through Witney, is its beautiful great green, right at the centre of the town.

Tours from Witney

Witney Tour One

Total distance: 19 miles.
O.S. Maps: 145, 158.

Outward Route

Leave Witney on the A40 road towards Oxford, forking right at Newland on to unclassified road for **Stanton Harcourt**. Leave Stanton Harcourt on B4449 in southern direction for **Standlake**. Join the A415 one mile after Standlake (in Witney direction), turning left on to B4449 to **Bampton**.

Homeward Route

Leave Bampton on the A4095, forking left after $1\frac{1}{2}$ miles for **Brize Norton**. Keep straight over the crossroads on the same unclassified road for **Minster Lovell**. Leave Minster Lovell in a north-easterly direction for Crawley, and cycle home on the unclassified road to Witney.

Stanton Harcourt. We loved this place. There's an air of peace and tranquillity here, and the beautiful old manor house, part ruined, had the Harcourt flag, yellow and scarlet with a swan, still flying. Pope's Tower, where he finished the fifth volume of his poem based on Homer's Iliad during two summers that he spent at the Harcourt home, is still occupied. It's an enchanting tower covered in roses, with beams and little windows. To get to the church, cycle along a lane parallel to the Manor.

The church is a must for everybody. Perhaps its most beautiful treasure is the flag from the battle of Bosworth. One of the Harcourts, Robert, was standard bearer to the young Henry VII at this battle which won the King his throne from Richard III. The flag, tattered and silvery with age, still hangs over Robert's tomb. Robert himself looks extraordinarily young, a boy with a serious face. Below him are carved some very worldly-wise monks and priests. An American girl was kneeling on the stone flags, busy working on a brass rubbing. (You can get permission to do this for a small sum.) While we watched, she produced a Norman work of art, a monk's figure all in gold on black paper. There was a little figure of a nun alongside which we would have loved to take home.

The Harcourt chapel, where the Bosworth flag hangs, has other Harcourt tombs which you must look at. As well as the Tudor Harcourts there are eighteenth-century figures with the elegance of the period, and a patronising nineteenth-century Harcourt statesman in his peer's robes.

Standlake. The country round here is flat and the cycling effortless, for you are in the valley of the Windrush and what is sometimes called 'the plain of Oxfordshire'. The river is much fished by small boys all of whom reminded us of William Brown and Ginger, and they seem to spend all day long on its banks.

Bampton. The houses are old, the school is a medieval grammar school and the town hall stands in the middle of a pleasant market place. The town is famous for its Morris dancing and we saw a whole troupe of the dancers, the men in hats crowned with buttercups and ferns, bells jingling at their knees.

Minster Lovell. The ruins are signposted the moment you cycle into the village. And so they should be, they are marvellous: the ruins of a great manor built in the 1400s by William, 7th Baron Lovell. He is buried in a magnificent tomb in the church, wearing armour, with the family arms, freshly painted in scarlet and blue, on the tomb's sides. His hair style is very like that of the young men of today, or of King Henry V.

People who enjoy sinister and horrific stories (that is most of us, when you see how horror films pack the cinemas) will not be able to resist Minster Lovell. It has two legends connected with it – both about horrifying deaths. One is the Mistletoe Bough legend of the girl who played hide-and-seek at Christmas time and was locked in a chest and suffocated. The other, more strongly based, is about Francis Lovell. As a young man he fought in the Wars of the Roses on the Yorkist side (for Richard III) and rose to high favour with the King who created him a Viscount. At Bosworth, when Richard was killed and Henry VII won the throne, Lovell escaped to Flanders. He returned to England two years later to fight in the Battle of

129

Stoke. The legend is that he escaped, swam the Trent and returned to Minster Lovell. He was hidden in an underground room and looked after by his old servant who died, taking the secret of his master's hiding place with him. Lovell starved to death, locked away in the cellar. In 1708 a chimney was being relaid when a large vault was discovered with a skeleton sitting at a table with a book, paper and pen in front of him. In the room was also a cap 'much mouldred and decayed' which the family judged to be that of Francis Lovell.

The ruins are of a very large and spacious manor house – you really do get the impression of its size and grandeur. The hall was 50 feet long and 26 feet wide, with great high walls. Many of these walls still loom above you, and there's a giant fireplace which must have needed half a blazing tree to warm people five hundred years ago.

By the neighbouring farm is the Minster Lovell dovecote which is extraordinary. It's circular, vast, of stone, and has a conical roof. The pigeons flew through a centre louvre in the roof, and the walls inside are lined with tiers upon tiers of nesting places. How simple we are in the 1970s, loving birds as we do. We thought this positive castle of birds was built because the Lovells were fond of them. It seems what they enjoyed was pigeon pie!

The Swan Inn here at Minster Lovell is a very attractive and elegant pub, a good place for snacks or a meal.

Witney Tour Two

Total distance: 32 miles.
O.S. Map: 158.

Outward Route

Leave Witney on A4095 in the Bampton and Faringdon direction.
At **Bampton** turn left on to B4449 for ¼ mile, then fork right on to
unclassified road to **Buckland** and **Buckland Marsh**. Turn right in
Buckland, and cycle ½ mile to join the A420, turning left in the
Kingston Bagpuize direction. After cycling 1½ miles, turn right to
Pusey House on the B4508. Retrace your route to the A420, crossing
it on to unclassified road for **Hinton Waldrist** and **Longworth**.

Homeward Route

Leave Longworth in easterly direction, after one mile you join the
A415, turning left for **Newbridge**. Cycle one mile, then turn right
into **Standlake**. Take right turn out of Standlake on to B4449 to
Stanton Harcourt and **Eynsham**. Return to Witney by the A40.

Buckland. It's an unspoiled place with a manor just at the back of
the church. The Throckmorton family built this rich-looking eighteenth-century house of golden stone. The family before them were
the Yates who lived in a tiny old house now the Estate office. You
can see their old home, and see them, too, if you visit the church and
look at the Tudor brass of John Yates and his twelve children – his
wife, looking like Ann Boleyn, wears the elegant Paris veil. There
are five prim little boys in ruffs and seven little girls in Tudor
headdresses. Buckland's church has a chapel with Pre-Raphaelite
stained glass windows, beautiful Rosetti-type women in opulent
Victorian colours.

Pusey House Gardens. This lovely Georgian house, golden stone, has
walled gardens, fine trees and shrubs. It's open from July 15 to
October 15 daily, also Easter, Spring and late Summer Bank Holidays.
There is a lake and a water garden, marvellous views, and white
doves fluttering around. We saw a white lace-cap hydrangea in
flower, and horses looked at us in a friendly way from over the hedge.

Longworth. Blackmore, who wrote 'Lorna Doone', was born in this village. Here too lived a seventeenth-century Doctor Fell who is still remembered, oddly enough, because an undergraduate wrote a mocking jingle about him. Reprimanded by the good doctor at Christ Church, he wrote something which has been used scores of times since in politics or literature:

> 'I do not love thee, Doctor Fell,
> The reason why I cannot tell,
> But this I know, and know full well
> I do not love thee, Doctor Fell.'

New Bridge. It's odd that this village gets its name from a 'new'. bridge which took the place of the old one 700 years ago! A beautiful chunky arch of a bridge that looks fit to carry traffic until Doomsday. It is, as a matter of fact, a village of two bridges with a pub at each end. At the Oxford side is the *Rose Revived*, a pleasing spot, and the inn sign is a pun, showing a big full-blown rose reviving in a tankard of ale. The pub gardens run down to the water's edge, and there are swans, white horses in the river meadows, and buttercups. On the Berkshire side is the *Maybush Inn*.

Stanton Harcourt· (This is covered in Witney Tour One.) As you ride towards the village, you'll notice the fields threaded with water – streams and rivulets which come from the Thames. Stanton Harcourt is beautiful and very quiet, its church reflected in a lake. The house belonged to the Harcourts and was a kind of fortress.

Eynsham. If you are interested in faint but recognisable medieval wall paintings, this church is worth a visit. There are pictures round the walls of the sanctuary and some of the windows. They're thought to show St Catherine's life and martyrdom and to have been painted by a Benedictine monk living at Eynsham Abbey. Wall paintings of this kind *must* be studied for a little while so that your eyes get accustomed to the shapes in the not-very-good light of the church. After some minutes you begin to see the paintings more clearly.

Witney Tour Three

Total distance: 28 miles.
O.S. Map: 145.

Outward Route

Leave Witney by the B4022 in northerly direction to **Finstock**, **Fawler** and **Charlbury**. Turn right on to B4437. After seven miles, cross A34 on to unclassified road to **Wootton**. Take the B4027 to the left, to **Glympton**. At Glympton take unclassified road to the right for ¼ mile, then fork left for **Sandford St Martin**.

Homeward Route

Leave Sandford St Martin by the unclassified road in Glympton direction. After cycling one mile, join B4030 for **Church Enstone**. Turn left in Church Enstone on to B4022 back to Charlbury, Finstock and home through **Hayley** to Witney.

Finstock. This village is set below the main road in a little dip. There are some new houses but you'll also cycle past cottages of typical Oxfordshire stone, greyer, not so gold as those of the mid-Cotswolds. There are houses of character here, and good gardens.

Fawler. To the south-east of the village are some sites of Roman buildings. It's worth asking about them if you are interested in traces of Roman Britain. But the village is unremarkable, although there are good views of hills and pastures on your way. The river Evenlode flows through the village.

Charlbury is also in the valley of the Evenlode and overlooks what's left of the great Wychwood Forest of the past. The country is gently wooded, and as you cycle into Charlbury you see it at a distance, its houses clustered cosily. We liked the look of *The Bell Inn*, dated 1700, and even the public library is a fine stone Georgian house. Wisteria stretches right along some of the houses in the village by the church.

Ditchley Park. Two miles north-east of Charlbury you'll find a really stunning eighteenth-century mansion designed by Gibbs. It is open from July 31 to August 11 in the afternoons from 2 to 5, and if you manage to do this cycling trip during that short summer period, do try to go to Ditchley. There are two fascinating lead statues representing 'Fame' and 'Loyalty', wonderful elaborate plaster ceilings in the Great Hall by William Kent, the artist in plaster work, and specially beautiful gardens. There's even a flower bed in the shape of the family coat of arms! And the woods and parkland are very fine.

Wootton. The village on the Glyme river is becoming very built-up but there are still pleasant corners to be found. We stopped for a while by the church which looks beautiful outside, creamy grey, with pinnacles and a square tower. There's a 1623 sundial on the outside of the church and fine limes and great yews, and hollyhocks grow against the walls. But inside it is severe and plain; history seems to have been swept away except for one or two formal eighteenth-century monuments. But we did like some angry little gargoyles on the top of the tower, peering down with their mouths open, soundlessly shouting at passers-by.

Glympton. A stream flows in a cascade, a sort of miniature waterfall under the chestnut trees. Glympton is thickly wooded, small, peaceful. If you call at the church, you'll see a life-sized statue of Thomas Tesdale, one of the fifteenth-century founders of Pembroke College, Oxford. He's at his desk, his wife beside him, and they wear elaborate brocaded costumes. There's a brass of the same Thomas on the floor of the chancel.

Church Enstone. The road is pleasant and open, with fields, cattle and distant woods. Elms grow well in this district, there are dry stone walls, and beyond them you'll see views of little villages in the distance. We passed an ancient barn where pigeons were nesting comfortably in holes made for them hundreds of years ago. *The Crown Inn* looked pleasant and the tiny church is castellated like a toy castle.

Witney Tour Four

Total distance: 22 miles.
O.S. Map: 145.

Outward Route

Leave Witney on the A4095 in the direction of Woodstock. After two miles, turn left to **North Leigh**. Cycle through North Leigh, fork right at the next junction to bring you back to cross the A4095 heading for **Church Hanborough**. Turn left at the next T junction after Church Hanborough to return to the A4095 for **Bladon** and **Woodstock**.

Homeward Route

Turn left through Woodstock on the A34 to visit **Blenheim Palace**. Cycle in a northerly direction for $2\frac{1}{2}$ miles, turn left on to the B4437. After half a mile, fork left off this road, through **Wootton Wood** to **Stonesfield**. Continue to **Fawler**. Half a mile beyond Fawler, turn left on to the B4022 through **Finstock** continuing south for $2\frac{1}{2}$ miles to **Hayley** and another mile home to Witney.

North Leigh. There's a ruined windmill in the middle of the village, and to find the church you must cycle a little way downhill. St George's flag flies over the church which is small and peaceful and has one of Oxfordshire's three Saxon towers. The Wilcote Chapel, which is fifteenth-century, is lovely, with pieces of stained glass, scarlet, sapphire and black, in the windows, and under a canopied arch, two life-sized beautiful figures in alabaster. Perhaps it is the stone which gives this couple their serenity. They are interesting too, because *both* wear the SS collar, which is that heavy chain worn in Tudor times by members of the House of Lancaster. It is very rare to see a woman wearing the collar. The lady has a formal garland round her head, with birds and flowers woven into it, and the man's head rests on a hollowed-out helmet with a marvellous bird on its crest. A dog at the lady's feet has the hem of her skirt affectionately in his mouth, as if reminding her that he's still with her.

As you cycle out of North Leigh don't be put off by the horrid-looking rubbish dump. There are lovely views after you've passed it.

Church Hanborough. Yes, it's another church to visit but has a rarity, a 'shroud brass' which shows on a winding sheet the almost naked figure of the first president of St John's College, Oxford. His name was Alexander Belsyre, who lived when he was old at the Rectory in the village.

Bladon. People come to this little village churchyard from all over the world to pay homage to Winston Churchill. He chose to be buried here in this country place with the rest of his family, including his father Lord Randolph, and his beautiful mother, Jenny Churchill. One would imagine that Churchill's grave, and indeed all his family's graves, would be in an imposing family vault or at least would have statues, carvings or monuments. But they are most simple and touching. Churchill's grave is edged in plain white marble, bearing only his name. Someone, surely a child, had put a small pot of marigolds thereon – the day we visited the grave; it was Churchill's only wreath.

Woodstock. It once had a great ruined manor, and Fair Rosamund was courted here by King Henry II, much to the fury of his beautiful queen, Eleanor of Aquitaine. But now it is a prosperous, rather substantial town, with handsome stone buildings and smart shops. We liked *The Bear*, which is an old inn from coaching days but very welcoming and even luxurious. The dining-room had crimson cloths, the lounges had comfortable sofas and reading lights. We stayed for coffee.

Blenheim. This is such an extraordinary and important place that we felt the only way to enjoy it was for the cyclist to know more about Marlborough, his captivating Duchess, and just how the massive Palace came to be built. For, noble and vast though it is, it is the people who lived here, their characters and passions, which must interest us more than the height of a column or the width of an eighteenth-century staircase.

Vanbrugh's huge monument to Marlborough seems at first just too large to touch you with anything but architectural interest. Or perhaps a little awe. Yet it is a touching place, it was a Queen's reward to the Duke of Marlborough for his victories, it was a gift to one of our greatest generals, a true military genius.

Blenheim

Queen Anne gave Marlborough the royal estate at Woodstock so that a great house could be built there for him. At the time there was an ancient ruined house there in a great, wild, overgrown park. Queen Elizabeth I had been a prisoner in Woodstock Manor's gatehouse. King Henry II had visited Rosamund there, it was said.

Marlborough was greatly pleased and moved by the idea of a castle being built for him, a symbol of his victories. But his tempestuous wife Sarah, Queen Anne's close friend, was less enthusiastic. At the time the foundation stone was laid, in 1705, Sarah sighed: 'I mortally hate All Grandeur and Architecture' and she meant it.

Everything started well. Work on Blenheim began enthusiastically and a thousand workmen were employed in building the mighty place. But after three years the money ran out. Sarah, indignant, considered the Government should vote her hero husband some more, and ordered the work to stop until the cash was forthcoming. She also began quarrelling constantly with the brilliant, worldly Vanbrugh, who was the architect of Blenheim.

By 1712 Blenheim was still only a shell, but work did begin again. Vanbrugh moved down to supervise the work and made his home in the romantic old Manor of Woodstock (which infuriated Sarah, who wanted it pulled down). But years went by, and nothing really was done again until 1716. By this time Sarah had got rid of Vanbrugh – she was a lady who removed people who annoyed her. Other people who had worked on Blenheim had vanished away by then. Some were dead. Others refused to come back and work again – Grinling Gibbons, responsible for the decoration of all the marble and stone, would not return. The Marlboroughs were at Blenheim when the Duke had his first stroke. He recovered but 'even to think of Blenheim', said Sarah, 'was enough to turn one's brain'. She considered it was a chaos which only God Almighty could finish.

In 1716 the Marlborough private apartments were at least livable-in. Vanbrugh had left, and the magnificent bridge he'd planned as a monument to Marlborough, a bridge 'worthy of a Roman conqueror', was unfinished. Sarah mocked at the bridge, fumed over the scores of workmen wasting their time on it. The cost of the Palace, up to that time, was £260,000, and Sarah wanted to 'put a stop to such maddnesse'. Marlborough had a second stroke, again recovered and was well enough to move, at last, into the house in 1719 . . . fourteen years after the work had begun.

Pictures, tapestries, furniture, were moved in enormous quantities. Sarah knew every stick and stitch of her vast possessions, down to her notes on '1 Chamber Pot the French fashion', and 'A Tea Kettle and lamp bought at Lord Cadogan's auction'.

In the summer of 1719 the family moved into Blenheim at last and did their best to liven up what Sarah had begun to call 'that wild, unmerciful house'. The duke was better and for a while enjoyed his noble home.

But Marlborough was not destined to die in Blenheim. He died at Windsor Lodge and was temporarily buried in Westminster Abbey as the chapel at Blenheim was not finished.

After her beloved Marlborough died, the Duchess was never fond of Blenheim. When she stayed there she used only one of its hundred rooms.

The tomb of the great Marlborough, and of his Sarah, shows him in Roman dress and the Duchess in her coronet, together with their two little sons. Fame and History sit at their feet.

When you have visited the palace, take a look at the grounds, designed by Capability Brown, who is supposed to have placed the avenues and trees to represent a plan of the Battle of Blenheim. The lake was made by damming the river Glyme, spanned by the bridge which Vanbrugh had wanted to make as an elaborate monument. In the distance you'll see the column of Victory, and a statue of the duke, dressed as a Roman, with a record of his battles at the base of the column.

There are marvellous Italian gardens, statues, topiary, roses and orchids to be seen.

Weekend Tours

Broadway Weekend Tour

Total distance: 57 miles.
O.S. Maps: 144, 145.

Outward Route

Leave Broadway on the unclassified road (north-westerly direction) for **Childs Wickham**. Turn left in the village for **Aston Somerville**, and turn right on to the A435 to **Hinton-on-the-Green**. Turn left out of Hinton and cycle on the A435 to **Evesham**. Turn right in Evesham on to the A44 forking left on to the B4035 and immediately right on to unclassified road to **Badsey**. Turn left in Badsey and cycle half a mile to rejoin the B4085, turning right for **South Littleton, Cleeve Prior** and **Bidford-on-Avon**. Cycle along the A439 into **Stratford-on-Avon**.

Homeward Route

Take the A422 out of Stratford to **Ettington**. Cycle on the A422 to **Pillarton Priors** and continue until the right hand turn for **Upton House**, a National Trust property. Retrace your route 100 yards, and turn left for **Shenington** and **Epwell**, bearing right at Sibford Heath on to the B4035 for **Lower** and **Upper Brailes**. Continue on B4035 for **Shipston on Stour, Charingworth** and **Ebrington**. Cycle to Chipping Campden and home on the B408, and right on to the A44 back into Broadway.

Evesham. This beautiful little town has already been described in a cycling tour from Broadway (Tour One). But there are many fascinating things to see, and we were interested to know more about Simon de Montfort, who died here at the Battle of Evesham. He was the first man to bring the middle classes into Parliament, and in 1258 he gained the support of most of the great barons and forced King Henry III to obey him. Over the next five years Henry gradually regained his authority, but Simon de Montfort rebelled and defeated and captured the king at the Battle of Lewes. But Henry's heir and eldest son Edward, who hated Simon, escaped, gathered an army and defeated him at Evesham in 1265. Simon's body was thrown down a well. Legend says it was recovered and buried in

Evesham Abbey under the high altar. The common people who had always loved him, revered him as a saint for a hundred years afterwards. His only monument here is a granite cross erected in the Abbey ruins in the twentieth century, and placed as near to the spot where it is supposed that he was buried. It's interesting that the English who have always been so law-abiding, revere two heroes who captured kings – Simon de Montfort and Cromwell.

There are many fine Tudor houses in Evesham; for example, the half-timbered Round House (we couldn't discover why it is also called the Booth Hall), and the *Crown Hotel* with its open courtyard. And don't miss the house, now the National Westminster Bank, also half-timbered and Tudor, which stands on a prominent corner. If you visit Evesham in the spring, you'll ride up to the town and out of it through the blossoming Vale of Evesham; its orchards in flower are famous.

Cleeve Prior. Visit the church to see the marks on the buttresses of the tower where archers sharpened their arrows in medieval times. You'll find more details of the church and the village in our cycle tour from Chipping Campden (Tour One). It's a pretty, quiet place, and in summer hollyhocks grow against the church walls.

Bidford-on-Avon. If you have time, you can padlock your cycle and go for a little river trip here; we saw many small boats. The town is rather undistinguished, a 'Dormitory town', but the bridge is very special. It has eight arches across the Avon, and a little way down is a ford where the Romans used to cross the river.

Stratford-upon-Avon. We've described England's most famous country town in our cycle trip from Chipping Campden (Tour Three). But if you have time on a weekend trip and arrive at Stratford on a spring or autumn day, you may be able to get a seat at the Royal Shakespeare Theatre to see a performance of one of Shakespeare's plays. This seems to us the perfect way to spend an afternoon or evening while you are in this part of the country. Shakespeare's plays, as well as their drama and poetry, distil a kind of essence of this countryside. Even the flowers mentioned in the plays still grow in gardens, fields and hedges, for Shakespeare grew up as a country boy and loved flowers. In our rides we have seen rosemary, rue with its yellow head of flowers, fennel, pansies, ragged robins (which he calls crowflowers), hemlock (which we call lady's lace), lady-smock, buttercups (which he called cuckoo-bud), and great hedges of lavender.

141

Stratford is full of beautiful places and interesting things to do. You can cycle to Anne Hathaway's little thatched cottage (at Shottery, only a mile away), see Mary Arden's Tudor farmhouse at Wilmcote where Shakespeare's mother lived, or visit Hall's Croft. Shakespeare's daughter Susanna and her doctor husband lived here and it's quite lovely. The garden is walled and there are some of the oldest mulberry trees we've ever seen, propped up like venerable old men and still bearing luscious fruit in the autumn, which stains the lawns bright red. You can have tea at Hall's Croft, sitting by a high lavender hedge and a long pathway edged with flowers.

Upton House. You'll need to push your bicycle up Edgehill which looms ahead crowned with trees. But the hill is short and sharp, and at the top there's an impressive and elegant mansion which shouldn't be missed. This is Upton House, a National Trust property, classically proportioned and standing back at the end of a long drive with lawns on either side. You can visit the house on Wednesdays and Saturdays, from May to September between 2 and 6, and during other months of the year on Wednesdays only. The gardens and grounds are beautiful, with terraces and herbacious borders, and in the house you will see Brussels tapestries, Sèvres and Chelsea porcelain, eighteenth-century furniture and a collection of paintings, many of them masterpieces of the British, Dutch, French, German and Italian schools.

Gazebo, Broadway

Cheltenham Weekend Tour

Total distance: 52 miles.
O.S. Map: 144.

Outward Route

Take the A436 out of Cheltenham in the Andoversford direction (east), forking left at Charlton Kings through the village of Ham and down the steep Ham hill to **Whittington** and **Syreford** (all on an unclassified road). At Syreford, turn left for **Sevenhampton** and, after ¼ mile, right for **Brockhampton**. Continue on same unclassified road until you join the A436 again, turning left to Naunton, which lies slightly to the left off the main road. Retrace your road back through Naunton to the point where the road joins the A436, and turn right into unclassified road to **Barton** and **Temple Guiting** ford (crossing the B4077) to **Cutsdean**. Fork right and climb Cutsdean hill, turning left at the top to **Snowshill** and **Broadway**.

Homeward Route

Take the unclassified road out of Broadway in a north-westerly direction for **Childs Wickham**. Here turn left for **Aston Somerville** and **Hinton on the Green**, at which point you cross the A435. Cycle on the unclassified road to **Elmley Castle**. Cycle on to **Little Comberton, Great Comberton**, cycling round the edge of Bredon Hill until you join the B4080 in southerly direction towards Cheltenham. In ¾ mile turn left into **Bredon's Norton**. After visiting, cycle through village to rejoin B4080, and after ¼ mile fork left for **Kemerton** and **Overbury**. Continue on same road to **Conderton** and **Beckford**, crossing the A435 and continuing on the unclassified road to **Alderton** and **Gretton**. Turn right in Gretton for **Gotherington**, and left in centre of village for **Woodmancote, Southam** and Cheltenham.

Naunton. There are many wild flowers and birds round here, for the soil is marshy and makes a good home for them. The village is on two levels and is built along a road which rises and dips, and the farms spread backwards from it – we saw one farm with a great barn and an ancient dovecote. The roofs are gabled, and most of them are covered with the familiar Cotswold tiles called 'slates'.

Temple Guiting. The setting is pure Cotswold, in the Windrush valley, and you'll see the beautiful manor farm which was once a summer residence of the Bishops of Oxford. The doorway of the church is Norman, and on the outside of the church are many delightfully hideous gargoyles. There are a number of Tudor stone houses on the banks of the Windrush.

Snowshill. The lovely National Trust manor is already included in our cycling tour from Broadway, number four. But it is so interesting that even if you have cycled here already, you'll find something curious or beautiful to enjoy on a second visit. For instance, in the room named 'Dragon' you'll find a portrait of Henry VIII in a fur-trimmed crimson coat and one of his favourite feather-trimmed hats. The big open fireplace (this room was once the Great Hall) also has the arms of Henry VIII on the iron fireback, and on the upper part of the walls you'll see the arms of the owners of the manor, dating right back from the Abbots of Winchcombe until recent times. The manor has been owned by three sovereigns – Henry VIII, his little son Edward VI, and his unhappy daughter Mary Tudor and her husband Philip of Spain. And in the room called 'Mizzen' are some Cotswold treasures of the earliest spinning and weaving days. Anybody spending time in the Cotswolds will be interested in objects connected with the wool trade of the past and on the table you'll see hand shuttles, fly shuttles, shears and carding tools.

Broadway. When anyone thinks of a Cotswold village, Broadway seems to come to mind. Its stone houses, wide grassy verges and the feeling of beautifully preserved antiquity have made it world famous, almost too much so. But you'll enjoy cycling up its main street, and you may decide to stop for a drink at the famous *Lygon Arms*, a seventeenth-century house which is now an inn and hotel. The doorway was built in 1620 and there are many treasures to be seen inside this comfortable and welcoming place.

Elmley Castle. The village is said to be one of the ten most beautiful in England. In the twelfth century there actually *was* a great castle here, the chief seat of the powerful Beauchamps. But the family married into the Warwick nobility and left Elmley in the thirteenth century, moving to Warwick Castle. Elmley began to decay; the stones were stolen, one by one, for houses and farms, walls and barns, and in the village church you'll actually see pieces of the castle masonry used for church extensions. The bridge across the Avon at Pershore was built from Elmley Castle stones. But the Deer Park of the castle still exists and deer still live there. At night they leave the park through gaps in the fence, and people in the village see them grazing in the gardens, the graveyard and the village playing-field.

Facing the church is a pleasant pub showing Queen Elizabeth being received at the village. The Queen came only once to Elmley and was entertained there. Among the dishes she enjoyed during her stay were roast swan, stuffed capons, suckling pigs, almonds and dates, venison, lamprey pie, partridge, jellies and sweetmeats.

The Savage memorial inside the church is a must. It is very beautiful, and shows three of the Savages – father, son and wife – lying together, carved in alabaster which has been gilded round the edges of collars, fringes of sashes, ruffs, and cuffs. The figures are dressed in Jacobean clothes and the Lady Catherine has her baby daughter in her arms. Two boys and two girls kneel at their feet, with serious but not unhappy little faces, the eldest boy with his hand on his heart. The family badge is represented, at the feet of Sir William and Sir Giles, by the mythological figures of lions and a reindeer's head, his throat pierced with an arrow.

The church is very much part of village life still, for there was a small exhibition of children's paintings in one corner when we were there – pictures of rabbits, robins and stout green trees. We loved the thirteenth-century font; around the base are four chubby dragons wearing broad smiles, while being crushed by the holy waters of baptism!

Bredon's Norton. In recent years the village has won four prizes for the 'Tidy Village' competition; it is very attractive, with stone walls, flowery gardens and trim cottages. Bredon Hill is in the distance.

Overbury. On your left as you cycle by, you will see Overbury Court behind grey walls, with magnificent cedars growing near the early Georgian house, in a fine garden and park. If you're interested in Neolithic, Roman or early Saxon relics, ask if you may visit the little private museum at Overbury Court.

Beckford. There was a Romano–British settlement here once, and Roman pottery, bowls and vases have been found. There's no doubt that there were Roman-styled homes here from A.D. 60 until the fourth century. There is a piece of fine seventeenth-century Dutch stained glass to be seen in the church, showing Christ carrying His cross. Another window in the north wall has Spanish stained glass. The yew trees in the churchyard were planted by the parish clerk in 1721.

Chipping Norton Weekend Tour

Total distance: 34 miles.
O.S. Map: 145.

Outward Route

Leave Chipping Norton on the B4026 in a northerly direction for **Over Norton**, forking left in the village for the **Rollright Stones**. Turn left into A34 for **Long Compton**, forking right on to unclassified road, and right again for **Whichford**. Cycle on the same road, turning right at **Stourton** for **Sutton-under-Brailes**; turn left into the B4035 and right on an unclassified road at the beginning of Upper Brailes where you will be signposted to **Compton Wynyates**. After visiting Compton Wynyates, cycle in a southerly direction, via Sibford Heath, joining the B4035 and bearing right immediately into **Sibford Gower**. Rejoin the B4035 and cycle to Swalcliffe, Tadmarton, and then fork right on to unclassified road for **Bloxham**.

Homeward Route

Take unclassified road south out of Bloxham to **Barford St John and St Michael**, then turn right into the B4031 to **Swerford Heath**, where you turn left on to the A361 for a mile, then right on to unclassified road into **Swerford**. Return to the A361, turning left into it, and after half a mile turn right on to B4022 for **Great** and **Little Tew**. Continue south on the B4022 to **Church Enstone**, crossing the A34 and forking right after a mile for **Taston** and **Spelsbury**. Cross the B4026 to **Chadlington**, where you turn right and cycle two miles, then rejoin A361 into Chipping Norton.

Long Compton. Although it's on a main road, it's a pretty and unspoiled village, with antique shops and attractive cottages, their gardens bright with tall flowers. The lychgate to the church has a tiny room above it with latticed windows, and the church itself is fourteenth century with a saddleback tower.

Rollright Stones. You'll find full details of these strange prehistoric things in Chipping Norton Tour Four. Do visit them – they're unique.

Whichford. It's a long pull up to the village but it's worth it for the wonderful panoramic views. By the edge of a wood you descend again on a humpy, bumpy road to the village. There's a big green, cottages all round it, and in the church is a stone tomb of John Mertun in alabaster in elaborate robes. You may like to stop for a glass of cider at the *Norman Knights*, a pleasant inn overlooking the green, which is comfortable and homely.

Compton Wynyates. The house has been called 'a jewel in pink brick' and it lives up to this rather precious description. It's in a hollow between hills and you'll approach it on a switchback-style road which has deep hollows and high rises but is certainly a beautiful, wooded route. There's a signpost on the left before you get to the house, which directs you to Winderton Farm for country teas. The ash trees which line the road gradually give way to oaks as you get closer to the house. From the entrance gates you'll have a fine view of this Tudor mansion which was once surrounded by a moat, and which has battlemented walls and twisted Elizabethan chimneys. The Marquess of Northampton lives here and it is open to the public over Easter, and from April to September on Wednesdays and Saturdays, 2 to 5.30.

The house was built in 1480 and stands in sloping Tudor gardens with clipped yews. There are roses everywhere and spacious lawns. On the entrance porch are the arms of Henry VIII and Catherine of Aragon, with her pomegranate badge which you can see embroidered by her own hands on a piece of altar-cloth at Winchcombe in the church. Walking through Compton Wynyates' porch, you see the square courtyard, you cross this to enter the Great Hall which has a minstrel gallery and carved screens. The whole house is full of marvellous things, paintings, panelling, Elizabethan ceilings and a very long table cut from one huge elm. The house has 80 rooms and is one of the most famous Tudor houses in the country.

Sibford Gower. The country road here is hilly and richly wooded, and we saw many birds flying out of the hedges. The village cottages are mostly thatched.

Bloxham. The village is high and the church is very fine, with a particularly graceful spire which can be seen for miles across the countryside. Among many beautiful things in the church, including a fourteenth-century screen, there is some pre-Raphaelite work – a big stained glass window which faces east, designed by William Morris and Burne-Jones, in the rich and typical colours of those Victorian artists, deep glowing reds and greens.

Swerford. The country here is hilly, and sheep graze in the fields as you reach the village which is built on a slope with houses at different levels. The lanes in and out of Swerford are so winding that we said it must have been called Swerford because you swerve so often!

Great and Little Tew. These enchanting villages have been described in our cycle tour based on Chipping Norton (Tour Four). Great Tew is specially attractive, a small village of thatched and stone cottages among wooded hills and orchards. We visited the church which is up the hill away from the village, and which is approached down a long avenue of lawns and trees, almost like a private garden. The church is surprisingly large and light, and as well as three sets of very good fifteenth-century brasses on the floor of the chancel, there is a monument to a handsome knight in armour, and a peaceful figure of a seated woman, Mary Boulton, near the high altar.

Taston, with its Thor stone, **Spelsbury** with its wonderful alabaster monument to the Lees, and **Chadlington,** a village with marvellous views and a stately manor, are all detailed in the cycling tour based on Chipping Norton (Tour Three).

Moreton-in-Marsh
Weekend Tour

Total distance: 55 miles.
O.S. Map: 144.

Outward Route

Take the A429 out of Moreton-in-Marsh north in the Halford
and Ettington direction for ¼ mile, then fork right on to unclassified
road for **Todenham**. Cycle through Todenham until you meet A34,
turning left on to it for **Tidmington**. Cycle through Tidmington to
Shipston. One mile out of Shipston take the right hand unclassified
road for **Honington**. Turn left in Honington on to unclassified road
for **Halford**. Turn left in Halford on to A429 (southerly direction) for
¼ mile, then fork right on to unclassified road for **Armscote, Ilmington** and **Mickleton**. At Mickleton, turn left on to A46 and cycle ½
mile, then take extreme left unclassified road for **Kiftsgate Court**.
Return to crossroads, fork left on to B4081 to **Chipping Campden**.
Fork left out of Chipping Campden on to unclassified road for **Broad
Campden** and **Blockley**. Turn right in Blockley on to B4479, continu-
ing until you meet the A44. Turn right, then cycle ½ mile crossing
A42, fork left on to unclassified road for **Condicote**. Cycle through
Condicote on same road, forking left when you join the B4077 to
Upper Swell. Turn right in village for **Lower Swell**. Cross A436 at
Lower Swell, taking unclassified road to **Lower Slaughter**. Bear left
in village, and after ½ mile turn right on to A429 (Fosse Way) turning
left for **Bourton-on-the-Water** which is clearly signposted.

Homeward Route

Cycle through Bourton to **Little Rissington**. Fork left on leaving
Little Rissington and continue until you meet the A424, turning
right along it for 1½ miles, then left for **Idbury, Bould** and **Foscot**.
Then fork left on to B4450, taking right turn for **Oddington** where
you join the A436. Turn right, continue for four miles, then turn left
on to the A44. After one mile, turn left for **Chastleton House**. Rejoin
the A44 back into Moreton-in-Marsh.

Todenham. There are good views here of the low hills of this rolling countryside. This is a Tudor village, with a manor house and a row of stone cottages which are small and charming. The old timbered school is now a private house. The church has a graceful spire with a weather vane of a cock on the top, and if you have time, take a look at the brass of William Molton and his wife, dated 1604, a year after Elizabeth's death. The couple look holy and prim in their heavy elaborate clothes. The old manor house in Todenham was once a rectory, and in the mid-1600s the rector worked on a Concordance of the Bible. Anyone who's used a Concordance will know what a piece of work he took on. It consists of listing all the parallel passages or actual items mentioned in the Bible (there's also a Concordance of Milton and Shakespeare). Thus you'll find all the mentions of rivers with their cross-references or all the mentions of King Solomon. What an immense work of love that must have been, taking the rector scores of years. His name was Wickens and he was ahead of his time – he published his Concordance 82 years before the famous one by Cruden.

Burmington. There are thatched cottages here, sweeps of cornfield, and you are high enough for good views of the hills.

Shipston-on-Stour. The houses and hotels here are mostly Georgian, for the woollen industry made this small town wealthy. The Cotswold tiled roofs are a beautiful colour and the whole town looks comfortable and trim. We liked the look of the *White Bear*, a Georgian-styled inn with a sign showing a fluffy young Polar bear swinging outside. And we saw some tempting antique shops. Shipston had a famous rector in the eighteenth century. His name was William Parry and his hand-writing was so beautiful that people mistook it for print. You can see some of his manuscripts at the Bodleian Library in Oxford. But there's no tomb to poor William at Shipston, which seems sad.

Honington. It's off the main road, and to approach it you ride through gate-posted pineapples, very different from Vanbrugh's excessively grand pineapples at Blenheim Palace. The bridge which crosses the Stour is elegant and odd, decorated with 22 stone balls. The village itself can be more truly described as 'Caroline Domestic' than Queen Anne, it's a delightful reduction in scale. The actor Ralph Hallett lived here and tells us that he grew gentians and wild iris and once stopped an otter hunt – he didn't approve of blood sports! The village is charming, with grass verges and little cottages with the church in a corner of Honington Hall's great park. We thought this church curious and rather gloomy. There are elaborate monuments to the Townsend family who lived at the Hall, and although the place is full of statues and monuments, on a summer's day it's empty and chill. You can see the Hall from the churchyard. It was built in the 1600s and is quite a distance away across rolling parkland through which the river winds; on the front of the Hall in niches are busts of six Roman emperors. We didn't know whether they were noble or wicked emperors but they seem a curious choice of guardians to the great house.

Chipping Campden. As you ride into the town you'll see the church which has delicate turrets, each topped with a small pierced gold pennant like a permanently flying flag. The high street is a beautiful line of old stone houses, many with velvety lawns in front. We liked the open Market Hall, built in the seventeenth century, with pointed gables and an open arcade; what a pity it's not still used as a market for the local fruit and vegetables. There's a ruined gateway at the end of the high street which was once the entrance to Campden House. The house was set on fire in 1645 by Prince Rupert during the Civil War to prevent Cromwell's army from capturing it.

The long high street is quite unspoiled, all golden stone with attractive arts and crafts shops including the Robert Welch Studio shop which sells gold, silver and steel jewellery in very contemporary styles, modern glass and vases and silver candlesticks, designed and made by local artists and craftsmen. At a tea-room nearby they sell local Cotswold honey. The *Noel Arms* in the main street is good to visit, with armour hanging in the entrance hall on the stone walls, and warm carpets underfoot. There's a bowling green at the back of the inn.

Campden recently won a prize for being 'the best kept village' and when you cycle through it you'll understand why. The wool merchants who made this town rich (we think it's too important to be called a village) were wealthy in the fifteenth century and you'll see some of their portraits in brass in the church. They are in the chancel and the one in front of the altar shows William Grevel, a wool merchant whose home, Grevel House, is one of the loveliest in the high street, with a two-storeyed bay window.

Broad Campden. You'll be able to see for 20 miles around as you cycle along here – there are panoramic views of hills, trees and corn-fields. The *Baker's Arms* is a pleasant stone inn facing clipped yew hedges, and the small old cottages are marvellously cared for.

Blockley. The village is on a hill and the church was one of our favourites. We visited it on our route from Moreton (Tour One) to see the Rushout tombs and the tombs of the Churchills related to Sir Winston. The church is one you shouldn't miss, the Rushouts are such a proud-faced impressive lot of aristocrats, and the Countess of Northampton is a redoubtable lady (she's the one who bequeathed bread to the villagers in the eighteenth century; it only ceased to be distributed 50 years ago.)

Bourton-on-the-Water. It's one of the most famous of the Cotswold beauty spots and certainly deserves more than one visit. You can see the model village at the *New Inn* or linger on the banks of the Windrush as it flows alongside the road, walking across some of the little humped stone bridges under the trees. If you are interested in birds (so many people enjoy watching them these days), don't miss the Birdland Zoo Gardens where, among other creatures, you'll see vivid humming birds flying free in a tropical garden. They're small, brilliantly coloured creatures who dart by, making a curious whirring noise with their wings.

Chastleton House (also covered in Chipping Norton Tour Two). Allow enough time on this weekend trip to enjoy Chastleton House. It was built in Stuart times and it really seems to have stayed untouched by the hundreds of years that have passed. It's a fine stone building in a lonely part of the country, set in a rather wild garden. It has many treasures. For instance, the ceilings are extraordinary – they are what is called 'plaster work' and look like decorated white iced cakes. We liked the beautiful pomegranate pattern with the fruits bursting open on the ceiling of the Great Chamber; below these were a row of painted 'Prophets and Sybils' with eerie faces staring down. There are many rooms to see.

Chastleton is still owned, on the female side, by the Jones family, who were devoted and loyal followers of Charles I. They still have a rare treasure, a painting of the king with transparencies so that in one case the king's head is held up by the executioner, in the other it wears a crown placed there by an angel. We spoke to the owners who say that if you specially want to see this portrait, and the Bible which the king gave to Bishop Juxon before his execution, they will be glad to show them to you.

The house is open all the year round (except Wednesdays) from 10.30 to 5.30, except Sundays when it is only open in the afternoon.

Northleach Weekend Tour

Total distance: 42 miles.
O.S. Maps: 144, 145.

Outward Route

From centre of **Northleach**, take unclassified road north-east to **Farmington**, turn right, still on unclassified road to **Sherborne**, cycle along edge of Sherborne Park, and on same unclassified road, to **Windrush**. Continue on this road to **Little Barrington**, and follow the river road along valley of Windrush to **Burford**. Follow unclassified river road to **Swinbrook**, cycling alongside the Windrush. Turn right, passing the Inn, then left at next crossroads for **Asthall** (unclassified road still) and turn left into the A40 (Witney direction) continuing until left-hand turn for **Minster Lovell**.

Homeward Route

Take left-hand turn out of Minster Lovell for **Crawley** (unclassified). After ¾ mile turn left on to the B4022 for **Hailey**. Cycle on, still on the B4022 for approximately two miles, turning right on to the unclassified road for **Finstock**. Bear left in Finstock and rejoin the B4022 for **Fawler** and **Charlbury**. Turn left on to the B4437, and after about three miles turn right on unclassified road for **Ascott under Wychwood**. Turn left on to unclassified road to **Ascott Earl**, to **Shipton under Wychwood** and **Milton under Wychwood**. Cycle through Milton, then fork left (running south) on to unclassified road passing old quarries on your left. Fork right at next junction and shortly cross the A424 continuing on unclassified road for **Taynton** and **Great Barrington**. Cross Windrush river at Great Barrington, turn right opposite the Inn for **Windrush, Sherborne, Farmington** and home to Northleach.

Farmington. The church is about 800 years old, and outside it is a little gem, but the interior has been almost too well restored, its beams smartly painted, its stone walls carefully preserved. But we found the famous little stone, a memorial to a rector of the sixteenth century, which has three symbols, each telling something about the time when the stone was carved – a tiny uprooted tree means this church belonged to a suppressed abbey, the drifting rudder (it looked like the large rudder of a rowing boat) was the symbol that

England had drifted away from the rule of Rome, and a Tudor rose, crowned, meant that King Henry VIII was now head of the church. You'll have to look hard to see this little piece of history which is above a small window on the left. We also found a small scratch dial near the door of the church outside on the wall.

The Pump House in the village, which is gabled, has a roof presented by the citizens of Farmington, Connecticut, in 1935 to celebrate the 300th year of the founding of that American State.

Little Barrington. The village nestles in a small valley, the stone cottages which cluster round the church are quite as beautiful as those of Arlington Row in Bibury. *The Fox Inn*, by the river, is very pleasant-looking, and your ride takes you past high beeches and willows.

Burford – Cotswold Wildlife Park. In acres of parkland, you'll be able to see many varieties of exotic birds, mammals, reptiles and a tropical marine aquarium. The park is open from 20 March to 31 October, 10 until 10, and in the winter only at weekends.

Swinbrook. There's another visit to Swinbrook in this book, a cycling tour based on Burford, Tour Four. But we felt that Swinbrook is a place that can be visited many times. The Fettiplace tombs are fascinating and justly famous. The effigies blaze in daylight, there's none of the dark mystery of some old churches here for the tombs are on the altar, and a great main window shines on their alabaster figures and shows, outside, a spreading view of fields and trees. The Elizabethan faces, some with pointed beards, are rather thin and elegant, the Stuart faces thicker and more pleasure-loving. The Elizabethans are formal, the Stuart alabaster is gilded and beribboned, but all the six Fettiplaces look cheerful and even smug. One can believe what one knows of them – that they married heiresses and were not famous for valiant deeds or for rashly joining any cause – even the King's. There's a fine Tudor poem on the wall which we copied down because we liked the sentiments of the wife who had it engraved there. It's to Sir Edmond Fettiplace:

> 'Whose native myldnes towards Great and Small
> Whose faith and love to frends, wife children, all:
> In life and death made him beloved and deer
> To God and Menn, and ever famous heer.
> In Plenteous plants by a most virtuous Dame,
> Who with his heire as to his worth still debter,
> Built him this toomb, but in her heart a better.'

At Swinbrook

Facing the river, at a turn in the road away from the church, is the very attractive *Swan Inn*, an old stone house covered with ivy and wisteria. You can stay the night here or stop for a while to have drinks and snacks. *The Swan* had a lot of flowers around and looks as if it has a landlord who cares about it.

Minster Lovell. You will find the *Old Swan Inn* ideal for an overnight stop. It's 500 years old, built in Cotswold stone – everyone's dream inn with bedrooms furnished in cottage style, and a large, comfortable dining-room with dark beamed ceiling. There is also a pleasant garden to sit in when the weather is good. A wedding reception was in full swing when we were there, so we decided to postpone our visit to sample the snacks that looked so tempting in the pewter-hung bar.

This village has great charm – the grey stone houses line the road, with wide, grassy verges in front. The bridge crossing the river Windrush dates from the fifteenth century; so does some of the glass in the windows of the light and airy church. We particularly liked a window on one side of the nave showing a doctor, in red robes, holding up a bottle – presumably medicine. The roof of the church is ancient, and the oak benches around the font are 500 years old. However, the pulpit and reredos are of a later date, around 1900. Look at the fine tomb of William, Lord Lovell, who died in 1455: his stone effigy lies on top of the tomb, wearing armour and long sword, his head resting on his helmet. Around the sides of the tomb are brightly painted shields showing the Lovell arms.

Minster Lovell is most famous for the ruins of Minster Lovell Hall. This was built probably between 1431 and 1442, on the site of a previous manor house, by William Lovell. His son John, the eighth baron, was made master forester of Wychwood for his services to Henry VI, and *his* son, Francis, the ninth baron and last of his line, fought at Richard III's side at Bosworth Field, escaping to Flanders and returning two years later to fight at the Battle of Stoke, near Newark, in 1487. His exact end is not known (see reference to Minster Lovell in Burford Tour Four), but his lands were confiscated after the battle of Bosworth.

Minster Lovell Hall, now in ruins, is most impressive still, with buildings ranged round three sides of a quadrangle. A huge hall dominates the ruins – it is 50 feet long by 26 feet wide, and 40 feet high – an enormous room to heat in winter, we thought, even with the open fireplace in the centre of the room. Part of the south-west tower still stands, now without its battlemented top but still showing traces of the original four stories. Nearby flows the river Windrush, making a peaceful scene.

Ascott under Wychwood. Shipton under Wychwood. These two villages, with their romantic names, lie close together in the Evenlode valley. We've chosen one item in each for you to enjoy as you cycle through them, as this particular tour covers quite a wide area of the country.

At Ascott in the church you'll find stone seats with canopies over them where the monks used to pray in the fifteenth century.

At Shipton, visit the *Shaven Crown Inn*. This is a jewel with a handsome Tudor gatehouse, a little enclosed garden and the unmistakable atmosphere of a house which has been lived in since the fourteenth century.

Envoi

A journey, to be a success, must have a purpose. In each tour we've chosen a town or village, some part of the countryside, some fine garden or little river which the reader may want to choose as his aim when he sets off on a morning's ride. Of course there are infinitely more things to be found in the Cotswolds than those we have described. That's part of the magic.

Index

THE RED GUIDES

Edited by Reginald J. W. Hammond

Barmouth and District
Bournemouth, New Forest
Channel Islands
Cornwall : North
Cornwall : South
Cornwall : West
Cotswolds
Dorset Coast
Isle of Man
Isle of Wight
Lake District

Llandudno, Colwyn Bay
London
Norfolk and the Broads
Peak District
St. Ives and W. Cornwall
Tenby and South Wales
Wales N. (Northn. Section)
Wales N. (Southn. Section)
Yorkshire Dales
Northern Ireland

SCOTLAND

Aberdeen, Deeside, etc.
Edinburgh and District
Highlands

Northern Scotland
Western Scotland

RED TOURIST GUIDES

Complete England
Complete Scotland
Complete Ireland
Complete Wales
Lake District (Baddeley)

Complete Devon
Complete West Country
Complete South-East Coast
Complete Yorkshire
Complete Scottish Lowlands

Britain
Portugal (Sarah Bradford)
Japan (William Duncan)

WARD LOCK LIMITED